TESOL VOICES

INSIDER ACCOUNTS OF CLASSROOM LIFE

HIGHER EDUCATION

EDITOR, **TIM STEWART**

SERIES EDITOR, **TIM STEWART**

www.tesol.org/bookstore

TESOL International Association
1925 Ballenger Avenue
Alexandria, Virginia, 22314 USA
www.tesol.org

Director of Publishing: Myrna Jacobs
Copy Editor: David Lampo
Cover and Interior Design: Citrine Sky Design
Layout: Capitol Communications, LLC
Printing: Gasch Printing, LLC

ISBN 9781942799771
Library of Congress Control Number 2016962180

Table of Contents

Series Editor's Preface ix

Introduction 1

Section 1: Voices from EAP Classrooms

Chapter 1 EAP Learners Explore Their Language Learning Lives Through
Exploratory Practice 7
Susan Dawson with *Phappim Ihara* and *Kan Zhang*

Chapter 2 Working the Problem: Finding Solutions to Student Dissatisfaction in
EAP for Engineering 15
Yasemin Kırkgöz

Chapter 3 Expanding the Boundary of L2 Literacy: Teaching Research Skills
in the EAP Classroom 23
Beatrix Burghardt and *Megan Hansen Connolly*

Chapter 4 Learners Deconstruct Classroom Experiences Through Critical Thinking 31
Asli A. Hassan, and *Roger Nunn* with *Hanan Nasser Salem Al-Hasani* and
Hanouf Ahmad Saleh Al-Enezi

Chapter 5 Formative Assessment to Promote Self-Regulated Learning in EAP 39
Saeedeh Haghi and *Gerard Sharpling*

Section 2: Voices from Language & Culture Classrooms

Chapter 6 Our Stories: Narratives for Culturally Responsive ESL Teaching 49
Debi Khasnabis, Coert Ambrosino, Saina Sajjadi, and *Catherine Reischl*

Chapter 7 Sharing Experiences of Intercultural Education Through
Student Autoethnographies 55
Gregory Strong

Chapter 8 Scaffolding Free Choice in Lessons: Negotiating Global Identity in EFL........... 63
Ekaterina Talalakina and *Idaliya Grigoryeva*

Chapter 9 Throwing Away Stereotypes: Deepening Intercultural Understanding
Through Cambodia-Japan Letter Exchanges.................................... 73
Nicole Takeda

Chapter 10 Pragmatic Development and Study Abroad: Building and
Maintaining Competence 81
Mark Firth, James Broadbridge and *Joseph Siegel*

Section 3: Voices on Approach & Collaboration in Classrooms

Chapter 11 Exploring Multiple Feedback Loops in EFL Writing Classes..................... 91
  Gordon Blaine West, with Sun A Kim, Juyoung Song, and Chae-eun (Cathy) Sung

Chapter 12 "I learn listening skill to get high marks": Student Voices About
Listening Instruction in Vietnam 99
  Nga Thi Hang Ngo and Hoa Thi Mai Nguyen

Chapter 13 Dealing With Resistance to Student-Centered Instruction:
The Struggles of a Japanese NNEST...................................... 105
  Ryan W. Smithers and Rie Smithers

Chapter 14 Teacher Collaboration in an ESOP Course: A Recipe for Success................ 115
  Akiko Tsuda and Darcy de Lint

Chapter 15 Students and Teachers Co-Researching Difficulties With Vocabulary
in Academic Writing: A Case Study of Exploratory Practice 123
  Qiao Wang and David Dalsky

Chapter 16 Conclusion: Theorizing Forward on TESOL Classroom Practice 131
  Tim Stewart

Dedication

For Isuzu and Kai whose voices resonate throughout my life,
making it all possible and worthwhile.

Series Editor's Preface

The *TESOL Voices* series aims to fill the need for expanding practical knowledge through participant research in the field. Each volume showcases the voices of students and teachers engaged in participant inquiry about language education. The inquiries of participants in various TESOL learning environments are told as insider accounts of discovery, challenge, change, and growth.

What constitutes TESOL classroom life and who is best positioned to research this unique ecology? Traditionally, there has been a hierarchy of credibility in TESOL encouraging the production of knowledge by credentialed "experts" in higher education who offer TESOL practitioners outsider understandings about teaching. In contrast, the *TESOL Voices* series presents insider accounts from students and teachers who are theorizing the practices of both learning and teaching for themselves. In other words, this series positions practice ahead of theory for understanding the complex phenomena of language teaching and learning. In short, the *TESOL Voices* series seeks to elevate the value of localized learning through classroom research.

In this unique series readers will discover relevant strands of theory extending from accounts of practice. The philosophical point of departure for the series is that enduring theory in TESOL is most likely to surface from participant inquiry that happens amongst the clutter of classroom desks and chairs. As participants tell their stories, reflective questions and implications for language teaching emerge that illustrate the practical theory practitioners use to make decisions as they experience classroom life.

The *TESOL Voices* series attempts to give readers a view from the classroom floor on the appropriateness of current policy, practice, and theory in language education. While the accounts in these books are personal reflections colored by particular contexts, teachers are likely to find parallels with their own situation. So as you read, listen carefully to discover what the murmurs, echoes, articulation, singing, humming, silence, cries, laughter, and voices that flow from each of the six volumes might teach you.

Insider Accounts from Higher Education

This volume featuring higher education classrooms shares insider accounts of TESOL practice by colleagues from various countries teaching and learning at colleges and universities. The volume contains 15 main chapters in three sections: voices from EAP classrooms; voices from language and culture classrooms, and; voices on approach and collaboration in classrooms. The concluding chapter situates the practical knowledge gleaned from each chapter within the big picture of contemporary theory and practice for second language teaching and learning.

Tim Stewart, Kyoto University

Introducing a Euphony of Voices From Higher Education TESOL Classrooms

TIM STEWART

T he aim of this six-volume series is to examine contemporary TESOL theory through the lens of classroom practice. Thus, the practitioner voices in this volume on higher education include students and teachers who reflect on how their teaching and learning experiences inform our current theoretical understanding. In the conclusion, I will describe in detail how the practice described in each chapter relates to current theoretical understandings.

Authors in this volume attempt to look at TESOL theory from the vantage point of the classroom floor. That is, they adopt a bottom-up orientation. This orientation is a conscious one in order to counter the temptation for grand narratives of teaching and learning theory in TESOL. Historically, such theories have been disseminated from the United States, Canada, the UK, Australia, and New Zealand. When planning this series, my intention was to invite voices from diverse classrooms. Consequently, you will visit classrooms in the United States, Japan, the UK, Turkey, Vietnam, the United Arab Emirates, Russia, and the Republic of Korea. The competition for a place in this volume was so great that I received over 50 abstracts for consideration. During the process, a couple of authors were unable to revise their chapters satisfactorily and withdrew their manuscripts. I have grouped the remaining chapters into three sections. Below, I briefly outline each one.

Voices From EAP Classrooms

Dawson, Ihara, and Zhang open the volume with student participants voicing their puzzles about language learning. These participants set their own agenda for learning by engaging in a process of exploration and discovery for two groups in the class. **Kırkgöz** took risks in her practice to respond to student dissatisfaction with traditional teacher-centered lessons. After consulting with subject-area specialists in the engineering department, she designed a problem-based EAP course. Her chapter offers ideas about how problem-based learning can be applied in EAP. **Burghardt and Connolly** stress the need to expand EAP programs beyond language skills in order to prepare students for the rigors of university education. They advocate teaching research skills that include a technology-based component. The voices in this chapter are of bewildered students from outside of the United Sates trying to learn the academic culture of the American university.

Hassan, Nunn, Al-Hasani, and Al-Enezi reflect on whether critical thinking skills should be taught in various cultural contexts and if there is lasting value for students in learning them. Their chapter centers on extensive reflections by two former course participants who explore how they view the value of their previous EAP learning in their current mainstream university courses. **Haghi and Sharpling** lament the fact that formative assessment is not used extensively in EAP. They describe a course that uses formative assessment as an iterative process and offer insights into effective feedback. Their chapter includes sample worksheets that illustrate how teachers might incorporate formative assessment into their courses.

Voices From Language and Culture Classrooms

Khasnabis, Ambrosino, Sajjadi, and Reischl tell their own narratives of learning in U.S. schools as immigrants. They see the stories of teachers and students as important resources for curriculum development. Their chapter describes a curriculum created through collaboration between university researchers and teachers in the school system that is based on the stories of both teachers and students. **Strong** illustrates how he uses autoethnography as a teaching tool in his English classes. As in the previous chapter, students write their learning stories, but the stories are structured around intercultural constructs for analysis. His overarching goal was to build a learning community where participants freely share their ideas. **Talalakina and Grigoryeva** highlight their different generational and professional perspectives on English as a Foreign Language education in Russia today. The chapter is structured as a dialogue between an experienced EFL instructor and a graduate student. Through their dialogue, the authors interpret the positioning of EFL in Russia today.

Takeda used letter exchanges to address stereotypes of Cambodia held by her Japanese students. Through this project, her students developed their intercultural communicative competence and learned interesting things about their own culture in the process. **Firth, Broadbridge, and Siegel** are concerned with the level of pragmatic skills of the students they send abroad to study. They contrast two students by analysing their progress from the time they began their studies abroad until six months after they returned. These students voice their opinions about the support they received before and after studying abroad, and their ideas helped to guide the authors in reforming their programs.

Voices on Approach and Collaboration in Classrooms

West, Kim, Song, and Sung explore their experiences with peer- and self-editing in an EFL writing class in South Korea. The three student participants wonder why they need to edit their work, and how to do it. The editing process is described in detail, and the chapter includes feedback worksheets as well as reflections on the process by the teacher and his students. **Ngo and Nguyen** describe the difficulties that teachers of listening encounter in rural Vietnam. Student voices reveal that current teaching practices and materials are de-motivating for many learners. Because the two authors are both teacher-educators and teachers of listening skills, they provide solid insider perspectives into current practice in Vietnam. **Smithers and Smithers** offer a frank and compelling narrative of a Japanese English teacher who struggles to teach in a student-centered way. Her perception is that the students do not value this type of practice. By researching her practice, however, she makes surprising discoveries that strengthen her resolve and open a new perspective.

Tsuda and de Lint serve up a collaboration between TESOL practitioners and subject-area teachers. Their chapter tells the story of how they developed a course based on more authentic student needs in a program for dietitians in Japan. Central to the course development was a wide variety of voices gathered through surveys and interviews. **Wang and Dalsky** share their experience of positioning students in their class as co-researchers. The educational philosophy underlying their practice came from Dick Allwright's approach to classroom research—Exploratory Practice. All of the course participants together explored a variety of puzzles about difficulties with academic vocabulary. Through these explorations, mutual understanding about course goals developed between students and teachers.

I hope the chorus of voices presented in this volume will inspire teacher-researchers to explore their practices systematically and share their findings in innovative ways with the rest of us.

....

Tim Stewart is an associate professor of TESOL at Kyoto University and the series editor of the six-volume series, *TESOL Voices*.

SECTION 1:
VOICES FROM
EAP CLASSROOMS

CHAPTER

1

EAP Learners Explore Their Language Learning Lives Through Exploratory Practice

SUSAN DAWSON, IN COLLABORATION WITH LEARNERS
PHAPPIM IHARA, KAN ZHANG, AND EUS 9 CLASS

"Why do I always speak English in wrong grammar although I know how to use grammar?" "Why does team 3 (which is near the door) always speak in Chinese?" These questions (among others) were posed by a group of 16 international postgraduate students during an intensive, high-stakes English for Academic Purposes (EAP) course I taught. They were raised in response to my question: what puzzles you about your language learning lives?" The questions spearheaded an eight-week investigative process using the Exploratory Practice (EP) framework (Allwright, 2003, 2005): a form of inclusive practitioner research.

This chapter recounts the experiences of two groups of students in the class as they formulated puzzles to investigate, collected and analysed data to understand those puzzles, and then presented them to other students and staff. I concluded the process by giving my perspective on their work. The chapter switches between the separate first-person voices of me, Susan (as teacher), and Phappim and Kan (as two collaborating learner-practitioners).

Context

The class, which I co-taught and in which Phappim and Kan were learners, was a 20-hours-a week English for University Studies (EUS 9) class at a private language school in England. It was for students hoping to gain a place in the institution's Graduate Diploma course (GD), giving them the opportunity to progress to a master's degree course at a British university. This trajectory was dependent on achieving an International English Language Testing System (IELTS) score of 5.5 overall, with at least 5.5 in each skill. For this reason, the dual aim of EUS 9 was to prepare students for the IELTS exam (12 hours per week) as well as introduce them to some of the academic and research skills they would need to successfully complete the eight-hour GD course. My remit was the latter, to introduce them to academic and research skills. The majority of the students came from China, with others from Saudi Arabia, Thailand, and Azerbaijan.

Course Objectives and Exploratory Practice

The language learning objectives for the course focused on the development of academic writing; planning of learning, time management, critical thinking, research, and reflection skills. One of the ways in which I sought to integrate these objectives was through working with the Seven Principles of EP, which is defined as an

> . . . indefinitely sustainable way for classroom language teachers and learners, while getting on with their learning and teaching, to develop their own understandings of life in the language classroom. (Allwright, 2005, p. 361)

In EP, all work for understanding should contribute to, rather than detract from, the teaching and learning processes in the classroom. To do this, every-day pedagogic activities become the tools in our work for understanding, making it an inherently sustainable and pedagogically relevant enterprise. The focus is on the quality of classroom life (Gieve & Miller, 2006) rather than technical problem-solving, improvement, or efficiency (as measured in terms of exam scores or progression rates, for example). The principles are as follows:

Principle 1: Put "quality of life" first.

Principle 2: Work primarily to understand language classroom life.

Principle 3: Involve everybody.

Principle 4: Work to bring people together.

Principle 5: Work also for mutual development.

Principle 6: Integrate the work for understanding into classroom practice.

Principle 7: Make the work a continuous enterprise. (Allwright, 2003, pp. 128–130)

These principles position the learners as co-investigators (alongside the teachers) in the understanding process, recognising that they too have the right and the responsibility to become the best learners that they can be. EP encourages them to pursue their own agenda for inquiry while getting on with the work of learning (Allwright, 2005). The principles build on Dewey's (1933) inquiry-based approach to education and Freire's (1970/2006) critical pedagogy, which seeks to empower learners and include them as active participants in a problem-posing approach to education. They also move toward what Kumaravadivelu (2001, p. 545) describes as a "post-method learner," that is one who is academically, socially, and critically autonomous.

My aim in using EP was thus two-fold: to foster a culture of inquiry in the classroom by allowing the learners to set the agenda, and to explore what was important to them; and to use the EP work to help fulfill the course objectives. These aims were based on both my own and others' experiences (see, for example, Hanks, 2015a, 2015b) of using EP with EAP classes.

Putting EP Principles into Practice

The way in which I interpreted these principles for my local context was to use many of the activities that constitute the standard fare of EAP classes in the exploratory work: listening to a lecture, taking notes, and writing a summary; undertaking a survey or research project; writing a report; giving presentations; and undertaking independent learning tasks and reflecting on them. While we also used typical EAP topics (e.g., innovation, crime, and punishment) to practice these skills, the EP work (to which we dedicated two or three hours a week) allowed the learners to refine some of these skills as they investigated their puzzles. From the 40 or so puzzles generated by the class (following an introductory lecture from me on EP), each student chose the puzzle he or she most wanted to investigate, and then formed a group with others who wanted to explore the same puzzle. The (unedited) puzzles chosen were:

- Why do I have so few ideas during IELTS speaking test?
- Why do I always speak English in wrong grammar although I know how to use grammar?
- Why I can't pay more attention in listening task?
- When I chat with foreigners, I feel more nervous and often make mistakes to organise my sentence. Why?
- Why does team 3 (which is near the door) always speak in Chinese?

Over the ten weeks, the students reflected on why they had chosen their puzzles, turned them into researchable questions, designed data generation tools, collected data and analysed it, presented their findings at a mini-learner conference to which other students and teachers in the Centre were invited, and wrote individual reports about the process (Table 1). The report and group presentations integrated much of the language work that we had done throughout the course and even incorporated IELTS-style tasks.

Other Ways of Implementing EP

It is important to recognise that there is not one prescribed method for "doing" EP. I have been working with the EP principles for several years, and the way the learners and I get started with "puzzling" varies. In contrast to the EAP example above, starting points in General English classes have included: a group-mingling activity based on different aspects of their language learning; group-brainstorming activities around what makes a good language learner under the headings "things you need to know," "things you need to do," "feelings and attitudes"; and general puzzles

TABLE 1. SEQUENCE OF EP WORK OVER THE 10-WEEK COURSE

WEEK	EP ACTIVITY
1	*Introductions, orientation*
2	Lecture on EP and note-taking, puzzle generation
3	Forming groups, unpacking puzzle, choosing data collection tools
4	Trialling tools in class and beginning data collection
5	Collecting and collating data, initial analysis
6	Start report writing ('methodology' — what we did and why)
7	Report writing — IELTS writing task 1 with data ('description'), peer feedback on writing
8	Poster making, report writing ('analysis' — what it all means and 'discussion' — what I have learnt)
9	Practice presentations, 'Learner Conference', final report submitted
10	*Exam Week*

(mine and/or the learners') that arise from everyday life in the classroom that we explore as a group, such as "Why are some students always on their mobile phones?" The process of working to understand the puzzles has (mostly) common elements: an initial reflection on why that puzzle is interesting; an unpacking of the puzzle to decide what we might need to find out to help us understand the puzzle more fully; some sort of "data collecting" process (using a variety of normal classroom activities); and sharing the findings within the class or beyond (e.g., class wiki, presentations, or a summary of the class discussion).

Phappim's Group

Our puzzle and why we chose it. I (Phappim) chose the puzzle "Why do I always speak English in wrong grammar although I know how to use grammar?" I joined with Eshrag and Bert, who also wanted to investigate this puzzle. Our reasons for choosing this particular puzzle were very similar: We all felt that we had studied a lot of grammar and understood how it worked. We also thought good grammar was very important for getting high scores in the IELTS exam. When we write in English, we have time to think about our grammar, but when speaking there is not so much time to think and to keep correcting yourself. This is especially true in the IELTS speaking exam, and we didn't feel we had always shown our true ability.

What we did to understand our puzzle. We talked about our puzzle and wrote a lot of questions about it, such as: where and when we thought we spoke grammar the worst, to whom, and so on. We then decided what sort of information would help us understand our puzzle. We made a questionnaire with both multiple choice and open questions. We spoke to students of different nationalities, and also some teachers.

What we discovered. We discovered that a lot of people felt the same about grammar, and everyone thought it was important to use correct grammar, especially in presentations and exams. Most people said the way forward was to keep practising and not worry so much about making mistakes. Some people felt they made few mistakes and said it was because the grammar in their language was similar to English grammar.

Challenges and opportunities. We enjoyed working as a team, and because we were from different countries, we had to learn to listen to each other, understand each other's ideas and, of course, we also had to speak English. This was a very useful experience and helps prepare us for university. Later, we were all in different classes, but we still helped each other when we had a problem or question. We learnt a lot about academic writing (it was a challenge to write 1,500 words in English, but a nice one), and also presentation skills. It also helped our critical thinking because we had to analyse the results and write about them.

These things were more important to us than understanding our puzzle. Sometimes in class we thought we were wasting time trying to understand our puzzle because we wanted to know how we could improve our grammar quickly before the next IELTS exam. We know we need to keep practising and have the confidence to speak to other people, but we still make lots of grammar mistakes when we are speaking and we didn't find a good solution.

Kan's Group

Our puzzle. I (Kan) worked with Vivi and Annie (who are also both Chinese), and we chose the puzzle "Why does team 3 (which is near the door) always speak in Chinese?" We had different reasons for choosing this puzzle. Vivi wanted to know if it helped students to understand the teacher better. Annie was surprised that teachers got angry when students spoke their own language, recognised she also spoke in Chinese a lot, and was curious to understand more. I chose it because I think that all international students find it hard to speak in English all the time and thought research into this puzzle might help us understand why.

What we did. Our class was divided into three teams (groups) around tables. We decided to observe each team for five minutes at a time, once an hour during class. We recorded how many people spoke Chinese, how long for, and what they spoke about. We also wrote down what was happening in the class at that time. We then interviewed other students and teachers to find out why they thought people spoke their own language in class.

What we discovered. The two teams with a mix of nationalities spoke little or no Chinese. However, the third team (all Chinese students) spoke Chinese in almost every slot. They spoke about the IELTS exam and the train times to get to their IELTS exam site. Once, they discussed English words in Chinese during a class competition. We found the main reasons people speak their own language is because it is easy. Also, because of a similar cultural background it is easier to find topics for conversation. Annie said that understanding these reasons had made her more aware of when and why she might speak in Chinese, and she was making a conscious effort to speak more English. We concluded that both teachers and students should work together to encourage people to speak more English in class: the teachers and administration can help by setting rules about speaking English; classmates can set a fine for speaking a language other than English and then buy treats for everyone at the end of term; each student also needs to regulate their own speaking and not just do the most comfortable thing.

Challenges and opportunities. The main challenge was doing observations in class because the teacher sometimes mixed the groups up, and we also had to concentrate on the lesson at the same time. We had to think about how to overcome these issues.

Interviewing students from other classes was a good experience as it gave us confidence to speak to others, and helped us to make friends with other nationalities. Working the puzzle helped our academic skills, and using our own data as practice for IELTS writing Task 1 helped us see the relevance of that test to our future studies. Repeating our presentation many times to different groups helped our confidence a lot, so we relied less on our notes each time.

Susan's Perspective and Conclusion

The high-stakes nature of the class meant that achieving the required IELTS score was the students' priority. In fact, many students were openly annoyed at anything not specifically IELTS related, and this included the EP work about half way through the course. I believe this overwhelming concern also accounts to some extent for the focus on finding immediate solutions (Phappim's group) rather than a willingness to work primarily for understanding (EP Principle 2).

If I were to judge the outcome of the work purely on the depth of understandings produced, I would be disappointed. In fact, this brought into sharper focus my own ongoing puzzle, and one which I am still working to understand: "Why is the pull of solutions so attractive to learners?" To try and understand this, I have talked to learners and colleagues, examined learner reflections, and investigated the academic and IELTS cultures of the learners' home countries. My thoughts so far include: the need for the EP work to be relevant to their personal academic goals; the self-imposed and parent-imposed need to succeed academically; student expectations of what an EAP course will help them achieve; and the pressure of a limited time frame (imposed by visa regulations and finances) in which to achieve their goal.

The EP work required a different way of thinking about teaching and learning. Learners are not necessarily comfortable with the ambiguity arising from "creating possibilities rather than certainties" (Morgan & Ramanathan, 2005, p. 155), and perhaps it is unrealistic to expect them to embrace (or appreciate) such new concepts within a limited time frame. It is interesting that in follow-up interviews a few months after the course, many learners said how useful the EP work had been in helping them develop a more critical, confident, and inquiring approach to their studies. As teachers, we might not see the immediate fruits of our efforts, but we might be able to plant something that can later flourish and grow: for example, a longer-term perspective on "quality of life" (EP Principle 1).

For this reason, it would be misleading to focus on the immediate product alone; the process itself is also a journey of understanding and development. Earlier, I cited Kumaravadivelu's description of a post-method learner as one who is academically, socially, and critically autonomous. In giving the learners time (even though they sometimes rebelled against it) and intellectual space to pursue their own questions, I observed hints of growing independence, evident in their reflections on the process. Academically, many discovered new strategies for learning and grew in confidence in their academic work:

> Before that I often feel fear on listening, because I always can't catch the point and afraid about that I can't understand, however through the puzzle I found that listening is not difficult like I thought. (Leo)

> It helps me learn some academic skills about research and understand the difference of essay between UK and China. (Annie)

Socially, some of the students experienced teamwork for the first time, discovered the importance of peer-support, and conquered their fear of speaking to students from other countries:

> The puzzle work has helped me to understand how important teamwork was. (Kan)

> Thirdly the presentation helps me enhancing speaking skills and not making me feel nervous or shy when speaking with other overseas students. (Vesper)

Kan's group showed the most critical awareness, questioning the use and role of native languages in class and recognising the mutual responsibility of teachers and students in reconciling differences of opinion.

It would be presumptuous to claim that these things could be achieved only through working within the EP principles, or that deep understandings could be developed within a 10-week course. Yet by integrating the work for understanding with the learning objectives (EP Principles 6 and 7), we were able to foster a culture of inquiry in the classroom that focused on the questions that were important to the learners themselves and in which they could work together to develop their own unique understandings (EP Principles 3 and 5). In this sense, the work contributed towards what Davis and Sumara (2006, p. 135) describe as the principal concern of education: "expanding the space of the possible . . . [and] ensuring the conditions for the emergence of the as-yet unimagined."

....

Susan Dawson is in her final year of doctoral studies at the University of Manchester, England.

Kan Zhang is currently working on his master's degree in IT in England.

Phappim Ihara is completing an MBA in Thailand.

References

Allwright, D. (2003). Exploratory Practice: Rethinking practitioner research in language teaching. *Language Teaching Research, 7*(2), 113–141. doi:10.1191/1362168803lr118oa

Allwright, D. (2005). Developing practitioner principles for the case of Exploratory Practice. *The Modern Language Journal, 89*(3), 353–366. doi:10.1111/j.1540-4781.2005.00310.x

Davis, B., & Sumara, D. J. (2006). *Complexity and education: Inquiries into learning, teaching, and research.* New York, NY: Routledge.

Dewey, J. (1933). *How we think: A restatement of the relation of reflective thinking to the educative process.* Lexington, MA: D.C Heath and Company.

Freire, P. (2006). *Pedagogy of the oppressed.* New York, NY: Continuum.

Gieve, S., & Miller, I. K. (2006). What do we mean by "quality of classroom life"? In S. Gieve & I. K. Miller (Eds.), *Understanding the language classroom* (pp. 18–46). Basingstoke, England: Palgrave Macmillan.

Hanks, J. (2015a). "Education is not just teaching": Learner thoughts on Exploratory Practice. *ELT Journal, 69*(2), 117–128. doi:10.1093/elt/ccu063

Hanks, J. (2015b). Language teachers making sense of EP. *Language Teaching Research, 19*(5), 612–633. doi:10.1177/1362168814567805

Kumaravadivelu, B. (2001). Toward a postmethod pedagogy. *TESOL Quarterly, 35*(4), 537–560. doi:10.2307/3588427

Morgan, B., & Ramanathan, V. (2005). Critical literacies and language education: Global and local perspectives. *Annual Review of Applied Linguistics, 25*(1), 151–169. doi:10.1017/S0267190505000085

Working the Problem: Finding Solutions to Student Dissatisfaction in EAP for Engineering

YASEMIN KIRKGÖZ

This chapter describes my experience of designing, implementing, and evaluating an innovative English for Academic Purposes (EAP) course based on the principles of Problem-Based Learning (PBL) for the first-year undergraduate students in the Electrical and Electronics Engineering Department (EED) of a state university in Turkey. The EED is an English-medium department, offering subject courses in the medium of the English language. The fundamental reason students choose to enter an English-medium department is to keep up with global developments to enhance their employment prospects, because most publications are in English (Kırkgöz, 2015).

The impetus for change and innovation in designing the EAP course described in this chapter is largely based on dissatisfaction expressed by EED students. Survey feedback I received from the students indicated that they were bored with their EAP classes because of the traditional teaching strategies that were used. That is, the lessons were mainly teacher-centered, exam-oriented, and followed a textbook. Students were dissatisfied because of their inability to find any connection between course tasks and their major discipline of engineering.

I am a language teacher with some background knowledge of engineering. Having heard the voices of EED students, I set out to design a course that would be different and innovative. To begin, I sought advice from engineering professors. My consultation with two such professors revealed that in their courses, students had to demonstrate abilities such as the capacity to solve problems, critically evaluate information, give oral presentations, and write reports on scientific topics in English. To support my students, I decided to design my course around the principles of PBL.

PBL has been used extensively in medicine. Its use in teaching EAP, however, has been limited. Wood and Head (2004) applied PBL to the teaching of an EAP course in biomedical English and claimed it was the first use of a PBL approach to teach EAP. Barron (2002) used it on second-year science students at the University of Hong Kong, and Prakash (2013) applied PBL to enhance the academic writing skills of first-year undergraduate English majors at a university in northern Thailand.

In EAP, course design often involves some collaboration between subject teachers and EAP teachers (Dudley-Evans & St. John, 1998; Stewart, Sagliano, & Sagliano, 2002). Collaboration enables both parties to take joint responsibility and ownership for the future direction of the problem domain, leading to the emergence of shared meanings and consensus by dealing constructively with any possible differences.

One type of collaboration is team teaching. Perry and Stewart (2005) investigated interdisciplinary team teaching at an English-medium liberal arts college in Japan where courses were co-taught by one TESOL specialist and one content specialist. They acknowledge the potential benefits for learning that a successful partnership can have on students and teachers alike, because the team teachers offer multiple perspectives in their courses.

During the development of my course, I collaborated with subject lecturers who were involved in reviewing problem statements, commenting on some technical points, and assessing students' PBL project presentations. I also took "the initiative in asking questions and gathering information about the students' subject course" (Dudley-Evans & St. John, 1998, pp. 42–43).

The questions that I hope this chapter will resolve are: a) Can I promote students' problem-solving skills in my EAP classes by designing a PBL course? and b) Can my collaboration with subject professors lead to a successful teaching venture? Through the examination of these questions, I offer suggestions for EAP teachers to consider about the place of PBL in EAP classes.

Building the Course Foundation With Problem-Based Learning Theory

PBL is an instructional method characterized by the use of real-world problems as a context for students to learn. The basis of PBL is a problem, or a query, requiring an explanation or solution (Walton & Mathews, 1989). The rationale for real-life problems as the starting point for classroom activity is to provide a meaningful context for student learning. As highlighted by Barron (2002, p. 308), "methodologically, real problems tend to engage students more."

Under the guidance of a mentor or instructor, students, as a group, define the problem, an essential initial phase in the problem-solving process (Harrington, 1995). Group members then identify learning issues, i.e., what they need to learn to resolve the problem (Hmelo-Silver, 2004). The students engage in a problem-solving sequence of collecting information from various sources, generating potential solutions, discussing findings, and considering consequences so they can construct a viable solution. Finally, they reflect on their experience, evaluating what they have learned.

PBL fosters several important abilities, including the development of cooperative learning, problem-solving skills, critical thinking, and communication skills (Albanese, 2000). The learners are positioned as active knowledge constructors who take increased responsibility for learning. Teachers serve as facilitators of the learning process, guiding and supporting students' initiatives rather than lecturing or providing easy solutions (Maudsley, 1999). Hmelo-Silver (2004) believes that PBL helps students to make their current and growing disciplinary knowledge visible, identify the knowledge gaps, collaboratively fill in those gaps, and then consolidate what they learned during the collaborative process.

In this respect, PBL is related to a constructivist theory of learning that is based on the premise that learners come to know something new by actively connecting it to what they already know. In other words, a learner's current knowledge is challenged, and through interaction with others, the learner constructs new knowledge (Maudsley, 1999). Assessment is based on the performance of how the problem is approached. These characteristics of PBL make it particularly applicable to EAP students' academic and professional lives.

The PBL approach is used widely in medical schools and in over 30 other fields (Albanese, 2000; Maudsley, 1999). However, its use in teaching EAP has been limited, particularly in Turkish higher education.

The Context

The participants were two classes of EED students enrolled in a one-year EAP program. Each class had an average of 38 students, all graduates of the Turkish school system. They had similar linguistic backgrounds in that they had received English lessons for the last 10 years. The majority of the students were males (average age 21). I taught both classes weekly for three hours in both the first and second semesters. Each semester was 14 weeks long.

In general, students' language proficiency corresponded to an intermediate level. The PBL-centered course is offered during the second semester. Because these students were actually receiving their subject courses in English, they were building up some specialist knowledge; I saw PBL as a vehicle for them to develop concurrently their language skills and specialist disciplinary knowledge.

Interviews I conducted with the students asking whether they would be interested in PBL revealed great enthusiasm, as highlighted by the student comment below:

❝ We have been studying English since primary education. We're bored of doing the same type of grammar and vocabulary exercises. Working on problems would be more interesting and academically relevant for us. **❞**

By bringing PBL into my EAP teaching, I could introduce EED students to a sort of "fresh" approach, in stark contrast to the teacher-centered, traditional approaches most students were previously exposed to.

Implementing a PBL Approach in EAP Lessons

I dedicated the first two weeks of the program to orientation with the philosophy of PBL. I first modeled the PBL process for students through an exemplary case study.

Following this, I divided the 38 students into groups of four to six, and each group had to identify a problem or case relevant to their discipline. To be acceptable, a case had to be relevant, have significance to the discipline, and require the problem solver to do research. To ensure that these criteria were satisfied, I previewed the problem statements from each group together with subject lecturers. The statements varied in length from 100–150 words, covering such topics as base stations, alternative energy sources, traffic jams, programming errors, and overcoming stress with electronic devices.

The following is a sample problem statement focusing on microwave-related issues:

It takes little time to cook in a microwave oven. However, microwave cooking is not natural nor is it healthy and it is far more dangerous to human body than we can imagine. It can even cause cancer. Because of this problem, we must reduce the negative effects of micro-wave ovens. We are going to search how to solve this problem. One possibility could be an electronic device. This device would get signals from the food, convert it into a value and give off an alarm. In this project, we are going to find out how technology can be used for the benefit of human health.

The students met in their groups to identify the main issues and formulate questions to work on. They generated the learning issues: the list of facts that needed further exploration. The groups began to solve the problem by asking themselves: "What do we know?" and "What do we need to know?" Students assumed responsibility for research outside the class on different parts of the learning issues. The groups then reconvened in the classroom and discussed what they learned, trying to apply the new learning to the original problem. To assist them, the university's librarian conducted a three-hour session to maximize their use of library resources.

Students completed a series of PBL activities based on the problem and the student's learning situations (Wood & Head, 2004). I carried out structured learning sessions to support students with relevant academic skills such as critical reading and academic writing skills, including paraphrasing, summarizing, compiling citations, and oral presentation skills. There was very little emphasis on language mechanics or form. The emphasis was on expressing the meaning of content that was academically relevant.

During the last two weeks of the class, students gave oral presentations of their work. At the end of the 14-week semester, they submitted their written PBL project. I collaborated with the subject lecturers for the assessment of these oral presentations.

Throughout the program, each student kept a journal in which he or she recorded a reflective commentary on his or her progress, personal skills acquired, the roles played by individuals in the group, and how their group resolved differences. At the end of the course, I interviewed students to explore their individual journeys of learning within the PBL program. In the following section, we hear the voices of students from the interviews and reflective journals.

Voices of Students

The main benefits that appear to dominate students' experiences of PBL are the authenticity of the learning tasks, development of language skills and disciplinary knowledge, and ability to cooperate.

Authenticity of the learning tasks. Students often pointed to the authenticity of the learning tasks as a typical feature of PBL. One student expressed this in the following way:

> ❝ After certain research, we agreed on anti-waves. This is an essential topic because when we want to concentrate on our study someone's mobile rings off and our attention is scattered. We're trying to solve this problem by inventing a machine. This device'll help us concentrate and we won't hear such disturbances in the classrooms any more. ❞

Authenticity was also framed as presenting students with the kinds of problems they will later encounter as professionals, as illustrated below:

> ❝ Our PBL Project is about one of the most interesting problems in business life: cables. This project is useful for me because I'm learning that bluetooth is a system without cables. Nowadays most companies have started to use bluetooth technology. So it's very important for me to learn about it. This will help me in my future. ❞

Students also found PBL activities highly relevant to their departmental courses:

> ❝ From the beginning it was clear that this project would be entertaining because we identify a problem within our interest. This project enabled us to learn detailed information related to artificial eyes. ❞

> ❝ PBL project helped us realize that you can actually use knowledge you learn in class outside. Preparing a power point presentation, working in a group is very important for our university courses and professional life. ❞

Language and knowledge development. PBL also offered linguistic benefits. It contributed significantly to students' language and knowledge development as they became more proficient in using the language of their discipline. Students benefitted from being "experts" on their topic and having to explain it in English. Below are some examples:

> ❝ While working on a problem I've improved my writing, reading skills and preparing a power-point. Most importantly, when I present my research, even though I may have talked in front of the audience before, this Project has increased my confidence. This is far more useful than having mid-term exam. I've also enriched my vocabulary. I learned a lot of electronic terms. ❞

> ❝ While researching on the project we translate from Turkish sources and at the same time learning about the subject matter. During this process grammar mistakes become minimal. While getting information from the internet, we express this information in our own words. My ability to produce sentences has definitely improved. ❞

This development is confirmed by the analysis of the students' first and final drafts of their project reports, which indicated progress on their language development. The first drafts of the PBL reports contained many linguistic errors. As their projects progressed, however, their linguistic and subject understanding, as well as their ability to express knowledge in English, greatly improved.

As proposed by the constructivist view of learning, students built on their existing knowledge when challenged by new PBL activities, which filled in gaps in their existing knowledge. This is illustrated in the following voices, which show that knowledge the learner must acquire is gained by having to complete a challenging project:

> ❝ Our project was about problem due to sitting a long time in front of the computer. While researching this topic my sitting posture has changed. I now have a different perspective towards computers. I don't sit a long time in front of the computer as before. I don't look at the monitor for a long time. I learned that the computer is not always beneficial. That's when used wrongly it gives people harm and physical problems. ❞

Findings are consistent with Barron (2002), who argued that as students explore different dimensions of a problem, they become engaged with the process of solving the problem. As voiced by the student below, PBL contributed to research skills:

> ❝ While working on the Project I had the spirit of a researcher. My perspective of looking at problems has changed. Everyone knows what a machine does but I'm curious about how it manages to do things and what is in the machine. We have also developed our research skills and how to organize information from various sources. Overall we have seen improvements in ourselves. We now know a lot more about the process of problem solving. ❞

Cooperation. PBL also fostered cooperation, according to the students who took collective responsibility for solving the problem leading to the emergence of shared meanings (Barron, 2002). The following excerpt is typical of many students:

> ❝ Preparing this project as a group has been useful in many ways. We've learned from each other. We come together, exchange ideas and combine these ideas. But sometimes there may be disagreements. We learned to have good relationship with each other. I believe doing a Project with a group is very useful. ❞

PBL also developed students' ability to think through a problem and analyse a situation. Students' feelings about PBL ranged from satisfaction to confidence, as reflected in the following extract:

❝ We worked on the effects of electromagnetic waves on humans and we learned a lot. We have investigated harmful effects of base stations and mobile phones. The general solution we have come up with is to keep away from tools that spread magnetic waves as much as possible. This is frightening as we always carry such tools with us. ❞

In summary, all the essential characteristics of PBL (Albanese, 2000; Harrington, 1995) were echoed by the students in this course. The course made it possible to combine student interest and academic relevance, while avoiding the duplication of topics and tasks done in their other classes. Using PBL in EAP classes raised only one challenge: getting the students to choose an appropriate problem and defining issues clearly, as reported by the interview extracts below:

❝ Initially, we had difficulty focussing on a problem. After identifying the problem, the second source of difficulty was to bring together appropriate materials and documents. We had a bit of difficulty in translating from Turkish sources into English. But thinking that during this journey if we had no challenges that road would take us nowhere we carried on with this Project. ❞

❝ At first I thought it'd be a difficult job, so it made me feel worried. What will I do? How will I do it? Can I manage it and so on? But as we went further I saw that I could do it and began to feel relaxed. ❞

Two subject lecturers I collaborated with commented that my approach was "innovative" and "unique," and that students were building up disciplinary knowledge within the EAP course:

❝ This course differs from other EAP courses in many ways. We observe that students apply academic skills they gain to departmental courses. Their communication skills in English has improved. So has their understanding of subjects. ❞

Conclusion

I have illustrated how I implemented PBL in one EAP course in Turkey. I now offer some suggestions for EAP/EFL teachers to consider about the possible place of PBL in EAP.

Second-language teachers should not be intimidated by PBL, because "lack of expertise or background knowledge is no barrier to this approach" (Barron, 2002, p. 301). Similarly, it is not necessary that the EAP teacher be an expert in the discipline, although in this case I had considerable previous experience in the area. EAP teachers can be specialist guides facilitating the PBL process (Dudley-Evans & St. John, 1998; Wood & Head, 2004).

Since the students themselves choose the topic to identify the problem, the teacher need not be a specialist to help them make the choice. A deeper benefit of PBL is that students and the EAP instructor can become co-learners, co-planners, and co-producers. Correct identification of the problem by the students can be confirmed by collaborating with subject lecturers.

My experience confirms the value of cross-disciplinary collaboration between a language teacher and subject lecturer. PBL in EAP/EFL contexts should be a collaborative venture. EAP teachers can therefore seek out the possibility for collaboration with subject lecturers to reach a common understanding and joint ownership of decisions (Gray, 1989) of various aspects in the PBL process, including the appropriateness of students' problem statements and the assessment process. Students benefit from the synergy of collaboration between the language expert and subject professors.

The procedures I followed in my course can guide course designers in other EAP contexts. Having successfully applied PBL to the teaching of EAP, I encourage TESOL practitioners to try it because it enriches students' learning of content knowledge while they develop their academic skills.

Yasemin Kırkgöz is a professor at the English Language Teacher Education Department of Çukurova University in Turkey.

References

Albanese, M. (2000). Problem-based learning: Why curricula are likely to show little effect on knowledge and clinical skills. *Medical Education, 34,* 729–738.

Barron, C. (2002). Problem-solving and EAP: Themes and issues in a collaborative teaching venture. *English for Specific Purposes, 22,* 297–314.

Dudley-Evans, T., & St. John, M. J. (1998). *Developments in ESP: A multi-disciplinary approach.* Cambridge, England: Cambridge University Press.

Gray, B. (1989). *Collaborating: Finding common ground for multiparty problems.* San Francisco, CA: Jossey-Bass.

Harrington, H. L. (1995). Fostering reasoned decisions: Case-based pedagogy and the professional development of teachers. *Teachers and Teacher Education, 11,* 203–14.

Hmelo-Silver, C. E. (2004). Problem-based learning: What and how do students learn? *Educational Psychology Review, 16,* 235–66.

Kırkgöz, Y. (2015). Students' perceptions of English language versus Turkish language used as the medium of instruction in higher education in Turkey. *Turkish Studies—International Periodical for the Languages, Literature and History of Turkish or Turkic, 9*(12), 443–459.

Maudsley, G. (1999). Roles and responsibilities of the problem-based learning tutor in the undergraduate medical curriculum. *British Medical Journal, 318,* 657–661.

Perry, B., & Stewart, T. (2005). Insights into effective partnership in interdisciplinary team teaching. *System, 33,* 563–573.

Prakash, L. K. (2013). Integrating creative problem based learning with authentic media and reading to enhance academic writing. *Journal of Education and Curriculum Development Research, 1*(3), 36–57.

Stewart, T., Sagliano, M., & Sagliano, J. (2002). Merging expertise: Promoting partnerships between language and content specialists. In J. Crandall & D. Kaufman (Eds.), *Content-based language instruction in higher education settings* (pp. 29–44). Alexandria, VA: TESOL, Inc.

Walton, H. J., & Matthews, M. B. (1989). Essentials of problem-based learning. *Medical Education, 23,* 542–558.

Wood, A., & Head, M. (2004). 'Just what the doctor ordered': The application of problem-based learning to EAP. *English for Specific Purposes, 23,* 3–17.

CHAPTER 3

Expanding the Boundary of L2 Literacy: Teaching Research Skills in the EAP Classroom

BEATRIX BURGHARDT AND MEGAN HANSEN CONNOLLY

Jiafan knocked on the door, softly. Beatrix invited him in and asked him to sit. The final draft of his final paper was already on my computer screen with certain paragraphs highlighted in red. "Do you know why I asked to meet with you today, Jiafan?" I queried. "I think there is a problem with my paper," he said, nervously.

He was right. There were several problems with his research paper, in fact: missing citations, insufficient paraphrasing, and content copied from Wikipedia. Throughout the semester, Jiafan had proved himself to be an engaged, friendly, and hard-working student. So I wanted to know what had happened.

This brief exchange took place during an eight-week intensive English academic literacy development course. As reading and writing skills instructors, we have witnessed student tears, anger, protest, and bewilderment. These experiences have taught us that our students need more detailed instruction to become truly literate members of the academy.

To gain a deeper understanding of literacy in ESL contexts, first we turned to Kern's (2000) definition of literacy, which posits that literacy demands the balance of cultural norms, frames of reference, and assumptions. Translating this theory into practice, the implication is that L2 literacy should "[draw upon] a wide range of cognitive abilities, on knowledge of written and spoken language, on knowledge of genres, and on cultural knowledge" (p. 16).

Following a developmental perspective, the ability to conduct research in English falls into three categories: 1) cognitive abilities, which can be interpreted as the ability of students to think critically about material and content; 2) a knowledge of written and spoken language, which can be seen as linguistic–in other words, can a student read a text and understand it? Can a student follow a lecture in English?; and 3) cultural knowledge, which we will interpret as a learner's knowledge and experience with the standards and expectations of the American academy (Atkinson & Ramanathan, 1999). To further complicate this framework, however, Weigle (2013) emphasizes that literacy development also has to take into account the medium of writing (e.g., a computer or pencil). If we stretch beyond traditional models of literacy instruction and assessment, we have to acknowledge that students must become literate users of technology.

Building College-Readiness in the Intensive English Program (IEP)

The academic skills class that we will discuss is taught regularly as a stand-alone course in an intensive academic English program at a large Midwestern university in the United States. The program prepares ESL learners for professional and academic study in the United States and provides instruction through seven levels. By the end of Level 7, students have achieved a proficiency equivalent to that of a U.S. high school graduate.

Since our program prepares the learners for entry into U.S. colleges and universities, we consulted the *College and Career Readiness Anchor Standards* (National Governors Association Center for Best Practices & Council of Chief State School Officers, 2010). This document details the skills expected from college-ready U.S. high school graduates. The writing descriptors for the English language arts in the document specify a component called "Research to Build and Present Knowledge," with the expectation that students are able to "[g]ather relevant information from multiple print and digital sources, assess the credibility and accuracy of each source, and integrate the information while avoiding plagiarism." The relevance of this component for our chapter is that it includes the skillful use of technology to aid students in learning to write.

Although research indicates that college professors expect their students to be equipped with the skills listed above (Achterman, 2014), empirical studies conducted with international student-participants (already admitted to a U.S. college or university) report a skills gap in these areas. For example, Cohen (2015) found that when students are asked to locate a book using the library's online catalog system, they spend only one to two minutes on the search. If they find something, they fail to check whether or not it is appropriate for their project. If they encounter any difficulties during the search, they simply opt to return to Google or YouTube.

Additional results from a survey by Martin, Maxey-Harris, Graybill, and Rodacker-Borgens (2009) revealed that students are not able to limit their search results and cannot interpret information displayed on the results page. International students also tend to check the results multiple times and have trouble understanding library terminology. These findings suggest that there is a need for a broader interpretation of "literacy" in English for Academic Purposes programs that will expand practice beyond language skills to include a technology-based research component.

With these considerations in mind, we added the stand-alone Academic Skills course to the traditional subjects taught in our intensive English program (i.e., grammar, reading, writing, and communication).

The Course and Student Demographics

The Academic Skills class is taught in Level 5, which corresponds to the 420–500 TOEFL score range (institutional version). In one section of the course, there are typically 8–14 students speaking different native languages such as Chinese, Arabic, and Turkish, among others. The learners arrive in the United States with a high-school diploma (at a minimum), which means they have already acquired literacy in their native language.

Adjusting to the standards of the American academy can be both problematic in terms of expectations and stressful for the students because the standards might be substantially different from what they are used to. Therefore, and perhaps not surprising, one of the main content areas of the Academic Skills course is avoiding plagiarism. Focused content also includes citations, the research process, and academic conduct. Students also compare sources found on library web sites versus a Google search to gain deeper understanding of search processes and search results. Specific course expectations are stated in the student learning outcomes (SLO) as follows:

1. Use academic search engines to locate sources.

2. Evaluate sources.

3. Annotate sources.

4. Use appropriate conventions of academic writing to incorporate sources (i.e., quotes, paraphrases, citations, and APA referencing style).

To allow for a hands-on and authentic research experience, we schedule each class in the computer lab. During the course, classroom interaction gradually shifts from teacher-guided practice to individual work to facilitate independence and accommodate the varying needs of our students.

To document student progress, regular in-class activities include the completion of a research log. This handout asks students to begin the project by recording their goals, then document their accomplishments and challenges as they search for and work with information. At the end of each class, they describe what they will do next. Finally, at the end of the course, students complete a worksheet answering the broad question: "What skills did I learn in this class?" Close examination of the responses given to these two assignments allowed us to observe the outcomes that we report below according to targeted SLOs. (We render student voices in their original form, including errors.)

Student Voices on Research and Writing

One of the topics covered in the course is the selection of sources. Once students have chosen an essay topic in the reading and writing class, the academic skills instructor presents a mnemonic device called the Currency, Reliability, Authority, Accuracy, and Purpose test, referred to as the CRAAP test (Blakeslee, 2010). After students have learned the principles of the CRAAP test and how they are supposed to use it to evaluate text-based sources, they try to practice these skills. As they explore multiple academic databases searching for articles, they practice limiting the search results based on date of publication and type of source.

Maria, who was working on finding evidence for the second argument in her essay and had already gone through a cycle of searching and evaluating the first source, wrote, "I finished the CRAAP test and it is a lot easy this time. I wrote the first reference." On the same day, Yilmaz found an article for his paper and stated, "I am going to review and take margin notes." These comments show that repeated practice helps students develop not only skills but also strategies.

When asked about challenges, Yilmaz reported, "I didn't know how to make citation from 2 same surname authors," while Emre, after searching for an article throughout the entire class-period, wrote, "I could not find some specific information that can use for my essay." Similar challenges were reported by others. These challenges indicate to us that learners are noticing gaps in their skills and now know the meaning of "relevance." These reports of accomplishment and challenges also suggest that as learners engage with their projects, they are indeed making progress towards SLOs 1, 2, and 3.

Answers given on the course-final worksheet provide insight into the skills and knowledge that students gained from the course. These were different for each student depending on their experience using computers. For example, Aliya reported, "I learned to read key suggestions, and I also learned to change the word to reach to what I want." This comment is important because it shows the extent to which the instruction about search skills has to be broken down and indicates that students need explicit training on how to generate and use keywords.

In other reflections, Yilmaz wrote: "I have learned how to select a good source with CRAAP paper; I have learned how to reach online academic libraries; [...]." Vera, from Venezuela, wrote that she learned "about plagiarism, how to identify and what it is, the CRAAP and how to use it."

Mohammed reported, "Computer skills is one of the most important that I learned in Academic Skills; I learn the good way for searching the Internet, such as EBSCO website." Overall, 33% of the students mentioned the CRAAP test by name, and 66% named the database EBSCOHost as a good place to find sources appropriate for their research. In these reflections, students articulated the designated SLOs by demonstrating knowledge of the tools needed to locate and evaluate information.

Every student made reference in their reflections to learning computer skills in the class. At the beginning of the course, we used the topics like "Mass media in everyday life: positive or negative effect?" or "Using social media for interpersonal communication: is it helpful?" to assess attitudes towards digital technology and to demonstrate how to locate and select sources using the library's database. In response to these questions, students readily took sides, with the majority voting for a primarily negative impact. Such responses suggest that, at the beginning of the course, they viewed technology as something that controls one's life rather than something that the user controls (Briggs & Makice, 2012). This understanding reveals an interesting parallel with the students' reported lack of success with searches at the beginning of the course. They frequently claimed that there was no research available on their topic, or that the topic was too challenging. However, we noticed that these perceptions resulted from typing misspelled words in the searchbox. A common response to this mistake, for example, was that students would rather add words to their search terms than check their spelling.

In contrast, at the end of the course we saw students carefully examining words as they accessed online journals and newspapers with ease. Maha is just one student who told us, "I learned how I can print HTML." Vera reported learning "how to organize an academic paper in Word, such as spaces and double lines" and also commented that "the libraries are not the useful places [they] used to be." These comments not only confirm that learners need targeted instruction in basic computer skills, but also demonstrate awareness of the changing medium of research in the 21st century. Today, most research has an online component.

The final product that demonstrates whether or not students have acquired the SLOs of the Academic Skills class is their research paper. This is a multi-source essay associated with SLO 4. We illustrate achievement of course goals with a paragraph and the partial reference list taken from Yilmaz's paper that addressed the negative effects of using social media (see Appendices A and B). Although the details have not yet been mastered, the format and content show substantial development in terms of following academic writing conventions, i.e., mechanics, grammar, rhetorical knowledge, and controlled use of document formatting functions to create appropriate academic style. The two excerpts reflect typical performance at the end of the course.

Finally, we reproduce two unanticipated comments that we were very pleased to read. Yilmaz stated in bullet points that "I got amazingly detailed feedback on my assignment" and "I saw how professors should be professional while they are teaching." These comments show us that when we engage students in acquiring research skills, they also learn values associated with academic conduct expected in the undergraduate American university classroom.

Academic Skills: Looking Back

The students' reflections demonstrate that introducing a research-focused Academic Skills course into the EAP curriculum provides relevant knowledge and skills for college-bound ESL students at the intermediate level of proficiency. The findings we present in this chapter both confirm and complement previous research. Similar to students in previous studies, our students struggled at the beginning of the course and were dissatisfied with not obtaining good results quickly. Our practice of engaging students in searching, evaluating, and incorporating sources over multiple cycles, however, seems to have facilitated success not only in terms of learning these skills but also in developing their understanding of research as a process.

The students also reported learning keyboarding skills during this course, which has been identified as an essential element of second-language writing and literacy instruction. Pennington (2003) asserts that it is necessary for ESL practitioners to incorporate technology into "the center of their own pedagogical practices" (p. 287). Indeed, Pennington cites research that posits that learners who are comfortable with technology tend to experience "less 'rewriting anxiety'" when using word processing programs, while producing longer, more complete documents. Our experience confirms the importance of hands-on technology skills in the Academic Skills course in producing learners who are not only comfortable with using technology but also appreciate the value of how technology can ease the writing process for university students.

The student comments led us to reflect again on Kern's (2000) definition of literacy. What we now see more clearly is the fact that all three spheres of literacy (cognitive, linguistic, and cultural) are necessary to conduct research at an American university. Most important, our experience has taught us that practitioners who teach L2 literacy need to consider the teaching of research skills as a stand-alone course. The Academic Skills course meets several of the cognitive requirements in Bloom's (1956) taxonomy, including analysis and critical interpretation, by deeply engaging learners in finding, evaluating, and synthesizing source texts.

Regarding the logistics of coordinating the Academic Skills course with the traditional reading and writing course, we also learned that close cooperation and collaboration with the instructor of the reading and writing course is essential for success. The goals for this sort of collaboration should be twofold: first, that the teaching of skills (like citation, for example) is repeated by multiple instructors, and second, that instructors in both courses have more time to concentrate on specific skills that improve the literacy of our students.

Academic Skills: Looking Forward

Essentially, we are arguing that a separate course in academic skills is both pragmatic and preventative. Our experience shows that this kind of focused instruction prepares ESL learners for the application of practical knowledge and skills as they conduct research in a college setting.

Since we are part of a multi-level EAP program, it is important for us to learn more about the possible effects of our practice. To do this, we consulted the instructor of the advanced level reading and writing course, who explained, "I am so thankful that [the students] already know about reliability, accuracy, and so on. I can focus on the notion of relevance in more depth. They are building on something they already know." This comment suggests that by offering Academic Skills as a required course we assisted not only the short-term success of our students, but possibly helped to create lasting knowledge that learners can use throughout their academic career.

Perhaps the primary value of the course in Academic Skills lies in its preventative nature. By this, we mean that with a targeted focus on skills and content, learners might avoid situations like the one Jiafan described in our introduction. In our experience, learners plagiarize not out of malicious intent, but because they are unable to use sources and conduct research correctly; in this respect, they resemble today's American college students, who Blum (2009) describes as more interested in sharing and converging than originality.

Our practice also aligns with Blum's (2009) conclusion that citation is "particularly unnatural" (p. 177). For our instructional purposes, we take this to mean that instead of a one-time exposure to the rules of academic conduct, we need to instruct our students on the conventions both in theory and practice. In short, we advocate expanding the boundary of L2 literacy to include the study of research skills. Looking forward, we envision the course to also include speaking and listening skills. This expansion would offer an opportunity for learners to practice research skills in various linguistic modes through a variety of media.

A further recommendation is to develop multiple reiterations of the course. The goal here would be to allow learners to interact with gradually more scholarly sources; such an approach can better prepare our college-bound L2 learners for what they will experience in the future and allow them to thrive in the American university setting. Our students face significant challenges. We know what most of these challenges are and see it as our moral obligation to ensure that we align our teaching practice in order to prepare our students for what lies ahead.

Megan Hansen Connolly is a lecturer in the Department of Second Language Studies at Indiana University–Bloomington.

Beatrix Burghardt is a Visiting Assistant Professor at Texas A&M University.

References

Achterman, D. (2014). The common core and college readiness: Part 2, writing. *CSLA Journal*, *38*(1), 10–12.

Atkinson, D., & Ramanathan, V. (1999). Individualism, academic writing, and ESL students. *Journal of Second Language Writing*, *8*(1), 45–75.

Blakeslee, S. (2010). Evaluating information: Applying the CRAAP test. Retrieved from https://www.google.com/?gws_rd=ssl#q=+chico+CRAAP+

Bloom, B. S. (1956). *Taxonomy of educational objectives: The classification of educational goals.* New York, NY: Longmans, Green.

Blum, S. D. (2009). *My word!: Plagiarism and college culture.* Ithaca, NY: Cornell University Press.

Briggs, C., & Makice, K. (2012). *Digital fluency: Building success in the digital age.* Charleston, SC: SociaLens.

Cohen, R. (2015). *Going straight to the source: What users really think of our catalog.* PowerPoint presentation at the Indiana University Bloomington Libraries In-House Institute, Bloomington, IN.

Kern, R. (2000). *Literacy and language teaching.* Oxford, England: Oxford University Press.

Martin, C. K., Maxey-Harris, C., Graybill, J. O., & Rodacker-Borgens, E. K. (2009). Closing the gap: Investigating the search skills of international and US students: An exploratory study. *Library Philosophy and Practice (E-Journal).* Paper 298. Retrieved from http://digitalcommons.unl.edu/libphilprac/298

National Governors Association Center for Best Practices & Council of Chief State School Officers. (2010). *Common core state standards for English language arts and literacy in history/social studies, science, and technical subjects.* Washington, DC: Author. Retrieved from http://www.corestandards.org/

Pennington, M. C. (2003). The impact of the computer in second-language writing. In B. Kroll (Ed.), *Exploring the dynamics of second-language writing* (pp. 283–310). Cambridge, England: Cambridge University Press.

Weigle, S.C. (2013). Assessing literacy. In A. Kunnan (Ed.), *The companion to language assessment* (pp. 62–84). Hoboken, NJ: Wiley-Blackwell.

Appendix A

Sample paragraph from Yilmaz's final essay

> According to Henig and Henig (2012) (p. 2), Ms. Henig has admitted, "I hate that sometimes I say something clever in real life and actually think, I should tweet that. Or that when my friend sends an email of a flattering photo he took of me, I get annoyed that he didn't post it to Facebook, where others could see it." That illustrates how people use social networks to get praises. Ms. Henig has also confessed that using social networks seems to increase her narcissist tendencies. She prefers the web sites, where she can talk more about herself and about her successes such as Facebook, Twitter or Tumblr. Davis, (2013) discusses the topic by saying that Users of social media actively take part in a kind of impression management, which modifies our concept of privacy. That is called 'Digital Other' (Chamber, 2013) which is usually used to protect and criticize celebrities, politicians in the public eye. Hence, it is almost a duty to be 'entrepreneurs of their own lives' for individuals.

Appendix B

Excerpt from Yilmaz's reference list

References

Chambers D. (2013) Social Media and Personal Relationship: Online Intimacies and Networked Friendship. *London, Palgrave Macmillan*

Davies, H. (2013) Online Intimacies and Networked Friendship. *University of Southampton, UK*

Henig, R. B. & Henig, S. (2012) The Torture of Modern Friendship. *Newsweek Inc. Volume 160, Number 17, P 40*

Latif, H., Uçkun, C. G. & Demir, B. (2015) Examining the Relationship Between E-Social Networks and the Communication Behaviors of Generation 2000(Millennials) in Turkey *Social Science Computer Review 2015, Vol. 33(1) 43-60*

http://www.chicagotribune.com/news/local/breaking/ct-chicago-weekend-shootings-violence-20160509-story.html

4 Learners Deconstruct Classroom Experiences Through Critical Thinking

ASLI A. HASSAN AND ROGER NUNN, IN COLLABORATION WITH
HANAN NASSER SALEM AL-HASANI AND HANOUF AHMAD SALEH AL ENEZI

I n the College of Arts & Sciences at an English-medium engineering university in the United Arab Emirates (UAE), first-year students, the majority of whom are Emirati, are required to take two communication courses, which we deliver through a project-based learning approach. We designed the second course to provide hands-on experience in using literacy and critical thinking (CT) skills through a semester-long project. At the end of the semester, students produce a full research report, a multi-media oral presentation and, in this particular case, a poster for public display.

The students conduct a research project on a topic of their choice in teams of four or five (in classes of about 20). This project consists of conducting a literature review, which includes composing research questions and collecting data using a combination of qualitative and quantitative methods. Our aim in applying this project approach is to provide a framework for developing academic literacy and to practice CT skills (see Bloom et al., 1956; Krathwohl 2002; Paul, 2007; Paul & Elder, 2009). These skills are especially important when students analyze and discuss their results.

We see our study as a way of exploring practice both as teachers and learners, with a particular emphasis on students' perspectives of their own learning experience (for more on exploratory practice, see Dawson, and Wang & Dalsky in this volume). We explore the nature of their narratives and give our reflections on the shared classroom experience.

Identifying Our Narrative Voices

Our chapter reflects the different perspectives of the four coauthors: two freshman English-language learners, a classroom practitioner-researcher (the first author), and an academic researcher-teacher (the second author), who did not teach the recorded class. The student voices appear in italicized extracts from their narrative reflections. As teacher-researchers, we are using the first person plural "we" to identify our joint narrative. "I" is used to represent the narrative of the classroom teacher (first author, Hassan). The second author/researcher (Nunn) has observed classes by the first author and has listened to the recordings and examined the transcript of the lesson we discuss here.

Our discussion centers on two short reflective pieces written by the student coauthors in which they reflect on the critical thinking skills they learnt in the course. In this way, it is the students' agenda that structures the chapter. We refer to samples of students' work and a transcript of classroom recordings to illustrate the process through which the CT skills were practiced. Our two student coauthors share their personal inquiries and reflective narratives of discovery and growth, as well as their views about the transferability of skills across the disciplines. Their perspectives on curriculum and pedagogy illustrate the ways they believe they have used these skills in other courses, such as their science and engineering courses.

Issues Surrounding the Teaching of Critical Thinking

In this chapter, we will also address some of the issues that have been raised in relation to teaching and learning critical thinking skills. Atkinson (1997, p. 71), for example, questions whether critical thinking skills taught in one context are transferable to other contexts. Other studies refer to issues related to second-language learners, finding that students use more elaborate skills in their first language (Luk & Lin, 2015). Le Ha (2004) warns that we need to avoid stereotyping non-Western students, arguing that the way local values are integrated into learning should not be regarded as a kind of "deficit." Akbari (2008), however, discusses ways in which critical pedagogy in ESL classes can transform the lives of second-language learners. Our own students are studying in an English-medium university in the UAE. By inviting local students as our co-researchers, we hope to show how students engage with the concepts we address in their own terms. The narratives of the two students include reflection on the transfer of skills from one course to work done in a different course.

Critical Thinking Skills in Theory and Practice

In previous studies (Nunn & Brandt, 2016; Nunn & Hassan, 2015; Yağcioğlu, 2009), we outlined 10 critical thinking skills developed from our reading of Paul (2007), Paul and Elder (2009), Krathwohl (2002), and Bloom et al. (1956) from an instructional viewpoint within a project-based learning context. In this chapter, we investigate the way students reflect on these skills (Nunn & Brandt, 2016), in particular the way they transfer them to other disciplines. Although the 10 CT principles in Table 1 evolved partly through interaction with students, the student coauthors refer to them not only in their own words, but they also refer to aspects of CT that were not in the teacher-researchers' repertoires.

The students who reflected on their experiences were from different project teams in my class (first author, Hassan). The reflections were written approximately six months after the students took the class, so we were able to see a metamorphosis of the skills taught and their long-term attempts to transfer these skills to other disciplines. Given space limitations, our chapter focuses on CT skill 5 because reference to this skill is prominent in their data. We will also make occasional reference to other listed skills (i.e., 1, 3, 8 and 9).

In addition to conducting a major research project, my students had to design a poster and present it. The topic had to relate to a freshman year experience such as a workshop, presentation, or social activity that they attended during the semester. They had to specify the target audience, the objectives of the poster, and the benefits for the audience in terms of the skills developed. I shared a rubric with the teams as they worked on the content of the poster. In our discussion

TABLE 1. CT SKILLS REWORDED FOR STUDENTS

1.	Look for opportunities for self-regulation to develop your own argumentation skills.
2.	Focus on relevance by referring to known information from literature in relation to your own projects.
3.	Explain your ideas and research choices.
4.	Focus on your choice of words to express appropriate levels of confidence in relation to your evidence.
5.	Develop the ability to analyse issues and problems (such as by breaking a task down into manageable components).
6.	Evaluate the strengths and weaknesses of arguments, research approaches, and conclusions (in literature for example).
7.	Interpret findings from your reading or your own investigations by selecting and explaining what is most significant.
8.	Develop the ability to synthesize output such as in group lit. Reviews or discussion sections of reports.
9.	Seek out opportunities for interaction with peers (and teachers) to develop your reasoning ability through dialogue
10.	Critically examine and proofread your own written output not just for language but also for coherent argumentation.

below, we draw on an audio recording of one of my lessons and the students' reflections on their use of CT skills. That lesson focused on the role of the audience, and, as the transcript (transcribed by the two students from the recording of my lesson) shows, I began by saying, "In your team, discuss what you want the audience to do, to think, to feel at the end of the presentation of your poster."

During the class, I felt that the students were comfortable discussing questions raised by me and their peers. The outside researcher (second author, Nunn), who listened to the recording, confirmed this view. I wanted the students to make connections between an audience that will read their written research project and an audience that might attend their poster presentations. During lessons, I kept probing for all the elements they needed to consider as they prepared their poster for an imagined audience. Students became deeply engaged with the project, and the classroom was fully student centered. As students began leading the discussion, I positioned myself as a guide.

We feel that this experience (and many others like it) might have enabled our two student coauthors to reflect in a very explicit way on a course they attended six months earlier. They also identified some of the core skills and practices that were developed during these interactions in the communication classroom. We do not set up this kind of experience in our classes as an end in itself. Rather, we see it as one component of a semester-long, project-based learning framework within which development of different types of skill sets is emphasized—just one of which is critical thinking.

Student Reflections

We will now highlight some key extracts of the reflections from our two student coauthors. They refer to some of the 10 critical thinking principles developed in our context, but only one of them uses the same lexis as the teachers' list (e.g., 'analysis'). The other skills that are indirectly referred to are the ability to draft a team-written synthesis from individually drafted literature reviews and the importance of interacting to develop thinking.

In the introduction of Reflection 1 below, we note that the student rationalizes these previously learnt skills. She gives her perspective about the meaning of critical thinking. Significantly, she raises the issue of transferring skills from one context to another, something that we have identified as a curriculum issue.

We also note that the student does address at least two of our 10 principles, but not explicitly. She refers to "synthesis" as "combining," for example. She also addresses the important role of interaction in the final sentences of Reflection 1, but not explicitly.

Reflection 1

❝ According to my experience, applying critical thinking within the course can either be easy or difficult depending on the level of application. For example, sometimes relating and analyzing the concepts of one section is very convenient to me while solving a problem, but challenges might occur when I try solving a problem at the end of the chapter, which requires combining the concepts from all the chapter's sections. Another example, by the end of the semester in the problem-solving-based courses such as calculus, physics, chemistry, and some major courses, I deal with problems that require combining and analyzing several concepts I learned through the whole semester. However, dealing with these problems is very rare as long as I manage my time because a previous preparation for the lectures creates a lot of questions and doubts in my head. Then, in the class lecture I get the opportunity to ask more questions and to clear my doubts. Hence, I have better understanding about the topic and clearer ideas. ❞

In Reflection 2, the same student develops the theme of transferring skills learned in one course to another. She adds the concept of "differentiation" from mathematics. She not only explains how it can help solve physics problems beyond mathematics, but also illustrates very graphically how important it is to seek out transferable skills learned in one course to solve a problem in a different discipline. The student's awareness of how these skills were being transferred from one subject to another demonstrates maturity and meta-cognitive awareness. It also challenges the perception that many teachers have of their students as unable to imagine situations in which they should transfer skills across disciplines. These reflections by students tend to confirm Le Ha's (2004) and Akbari's (2008) beliefs that we should not stereotype ESL students or pre-judge what they are able to do.

Reflection 2

❝ Another case in which I have to apply critical thinking is when I have to connect the knowledge I got from one course to a topic in another course. Some of my peers find this practice very challenging. I also find this somehow challenging just in the beginning of the courses, because at that time I have my focus all concentrated on learning and remembering the fresh concepts I'm taking in the new course. I can represent this case in someone who has all the ingredients to make cinnamon buns but does not know how to prepare them. For example, in the beginning of my physics course, I once tried to solve a problem which asked for finding the maximum force that acts on an electric charge in an electric field. I was stuck on how to solve this problem because solving it requires differentiation, a method of solving problems to find extremes I took in my first calculus course one year ago. Unfortunately, even that I knew how to differentiate an equation, I couldn't think of that method because I was only searching for physical equations I took in this physics course that will directly give me the answer. Dealing with combining information from different courses sound scary to me but only few practicing work out the issue. Indeed I found myself knowing all the mathematical method that I have to use in physics course. . . . However, I notice that the trouble with combining different courses material was only an expectation problem because when I try solving a physical problem and stuck on it I never expect of calculus to help me solve it. Nevertheless, in the middle of the course, after few practicing, I can easily identify if solving a problem requires bringing up what I have taken in my calculus course and the previous physics courses. **"**

In Reflection 3, the second student addresses writing as one of the skill areas in which she improved during her time in the class. She gives details of all the types of writing she did, specifically focusing on the individual writing experiences such as writing a literature review (Nunn, Deveci, & Salih, 2015) for the research project that helped later in writing a book report for another class.

She mentioned that the difference between expressing her own opinions as opposed to the opinion of an expert was one of the hardest concepts to master in argumentation writing (Nunn & Hassan, 2015). Students are constantly told that they need to support their ideas with evidence.

Reflection 3

" Another challenging skill that we have gained was the writing skill. In the communication class, we were taught how to write technical reports. The technical writing is used in variety of technical and working fields in which it focuses on providing information. The technical report is characterized by being formal, includes only the main points and doesn't include our personal feelings. In addition, we should be specific and make sure to include citations and not a lot of quotes. One of the things that we have taken in the course was the literature review. Writing literature reviews helped us in another course where the instructor assigned us to write a book review. In communication classes, we covered writing reviews, citation, and paraphrasing in which I utilized what I learned to write a book review for the other course. **"**

In Reflection 4, the student explicitly refers to 'analysis' (CT skill 5).

Reflection 4

" COMM151 might not be a problem solving based course, but I applied a lot of critical thinking in this course when I was working in my group research. This helped me quite develop my critical thinking skills. As a result, I find applying critical thinking in other course not quite difficult because it is based on knowing the roots of the problem then analyzing the problem to work out the solution. I learned or realized this scheme of applying critical thinking to solve a problem only in the COMM151 course. . . . Thus, using and developing my critical thinking is much easier now after I follow the scheme that I learned from COMM151.

In conclusion, I see the work I did in the COMM151 course a good training of critical thinking, the skill that I think is the most important in my department. The only challenges that rise now when I apply critical thinking are easy to overcome since they only need some time management, preparations, better expectations and few practicing. **"**

Conclusion

In a response to Atkinson's (1997) contrary claim, our chapter highlights our students' perspectives on the importance of transferring skills learnt in one context to another. It is important to note that the students' reflections, which make up a substantial part of this chapter, were intentionally written six months after the classes ended. The reflection process seems to have provided an opportunity for the two students to gauge the degree to which the professional "soft" skills introduced in the communication classroom were transferred to other disciplines.

While the focus of our discussion is on the students' contributions and reflections, the reflective approach provided space for us to think back on shared learning experiences. Perhaps the best pedagogical response to researchers like Atkinson is for practitioners to resist imposing solutions found in the general literature, striving instead to make conscious adjustments to their teaching practices by learning more about the values present in the local context (Le Ha, 2004). By working collaboratively with local students, we became aware of the way students transferred the skills learned in our class to other classes.

The exploration of practice we have presented was a collaborative effort between teacher-researchers and students. Clearly, students have a vital role in helping us understand the learning that goes on in our classrooms. As expatriate teachers, we must make our students aware that we value their cultures and their ideas. By soliciting students' voices through classroom research, practitioners can add a new dimension to learner-centered classrooms.

Dr. Asli Hassan is Assistant Professor of Communication at the Petroleum Institute, Abu Dhabi.

Dr. Roger Nunn is Professor of Communication at the Petroleum Institute, Abu Dhabi.

Hanan Nasser Salem Al-Hasani is a student of Chemical Engineering at the Petroleum Institute, Abu Dhabi.

Hanouf Ahmad Saleh Al Enezi is a student of Mechanical Engineering at the Petroleum Institute, Abu Dhabi.

References

Akbari, R. (2008). Transforming lives: introducing critical pedagogy into ELT classrooms. *ELT Journal*, 62(3), 276–283.

Atkinson, D. (1997). A critical approach to critical thinking in TESOL. *TESOL Quarterly*, 31(1), 71–94.

Bloom, B. S., Engelhart, M. D., Furst, E. J., Hill, W. H., & Krathwohl, D. R. (1956). *Taxonomy of educational objectives: The classification of educational goals.* Handbook I: Cognitive domain. New York, NY: David McKay Company.

Krathwohl, D. R. (2002). 'A revision of Bloom's Taxonomy: An overview.' *Theory into Practice*, 41(4), 212.

Le Ha, P. (2004). University classrooms in Vietnam: Contesting the stereotypes. *ELT Journal*, 58(1), 50–57.

Luk, J., & Lin, A. (2015). Voices without words: Doing critical literate talk in English as a Second Language. *TESOL Quarterly*, 49(1), 67–91.

Nunn, R., &. Brandt, C. (2016). A phenomenological approach to reflective writing, *English Scholarship Beyond Borders*, 2(1), 130–151.

Nunn, R., & Hassan, A. (2015). Investigating the teaching of critical reasoning using 'method-in-use' protocols: A trial lesson analysis. In V. Reddy (Ed.), *Papers in language teaching and learning: In honour of Professor Z. N. Patil.* New Delhi, India: Allied Publishers.

Nunn, R., Deveci, T., & Salih, H. (2015). Phenomenological views of the development of critical argumentation in learners' discourse. *Asian EFL Journal, 85,* 90–116.

Paul, R. (2007). Critical thinking in every domain of knowledge and belief. *27th Annual International Conference on Critical Thinking.* Retrieved from: http://www.criticalthinking.org /pages/critical-thinking-in-every-domain-of-knowledge-and-belief/698

Paul, R., & Elder, L. (2009). *The miniature guide to critical thinking: Concept and tools.* Dillon Beach, CA: Foundation for Critical Thinking Press.

Yağcioğlu, Ö. (2009). Critical thinking and task-based learning in teaching reading courses at Dokuz Eylul University in Turkey. *Ekev Academic Review, 13*(38), 287–298.

5 Formative Assessment to Promote Self-Regulated Learning in EAP

SAEEDEH HAGHI AND GERARD SHARPLING

M ost methods of assessment used in English for academic purposes (EAP) courses in the UK seem to be mainly teacher oriented, i.e., summative with few formative features, particularly students' involvement (Banerjee & Wall, 2006). This chapter addresses the question: "How might students react to a course that incorporates formative assessments?"

In recent years, studies of assessment show a growing interest in the interactions between assessment, learning, and teaching practices. The use of assessment is no longer confined to measuring learners' achievement; it is also used as a means of providing information that can facilitate learning and instructional practices. Assessments such as these are known as "formative assessments" (William & Black, 1998).

Formative assessment (FA) is regarded as a powerful method of enhancing student achievement. "Formative assessment and formative feedback are very powerful and potentially constructive learning tools" (Irons, 2008, p. 135). FA, which can be contrasted with summative assessment, is used in the evaluation of a learner's learning process—assessment *for* learning. While summative assessment, or assessment *of* learning, provides a snapshot of a student's achievement, FA functions as an iterative process, with feedback loops as its central component, assisting students as their learning progresses.

In this chapter, we describe FA as any task that can provide teachers and students with feedback that might reduce the gap between learners' current level of achievement and the desired level of achievement.

Features of Formative Assessment

While teaching English for academic purposes over the past few years, I (first author, Haghi) assumed that giving regular tests to students and merely informing them of the results is an acceptable way to practice FA. It was during my involvement in a postgraduate studies project, however, when I noticed that, in fact, "formative assessment is not an instrument or an event, but a collection of practices with a common feature: they all lead to some *action* that improves learning" (Chappuis, 2007, p. 4). In this project, supervised by the second author (Sharpling), who was my graduate supervisor at the time, I became familiar with several frameworks that address salient features of FA. Heritage's (2010) formative assessment model, for example, suggests guidelines for appropriate implementation of FA. In this model, there are four key elements of the FA process: learning progressions (learning objectives and success criteria, identifying the learning gap, and learning evidence); teacher assessment; effective feedback; and learner involvement.

Sadler's model (1989) suggests three conditions for "assessment *for* learning." According to this model, effective FA should enable learners to answer three questions in relation to their learning: 1. "Where are you trying to go?," 2. "Where are you now?," and 3. "How can you get there?" Setting learning objectives and success criteria will help learners explore their learning goals and pathways.

The Importance of Feedback

A key component of FA I learned about was feedback, which is one of the key conditions of assessment for learning. According to the research, feedback is crucial in learning achievement (Epstein et al., 2002; Moreno, 2004). For example, in Hattie's (1999) effect size list, feedback falls into the top 10 influences on students' learning and achievement. It is important to note that there is variability in the power of different feedback types. According to Hattie's list, the most purposeful are those that provide students with information about a task, and ways and processes for improving future performance.

Prior to this project, the feedback my students received was limited to some written comments on their work (e.g., their essays). I discovered that by only giving students some feedback on their work, with no follow up to see how students act on the feedback I provided, I was not practicing FA correctly. In addition, I realized that in order for my feedback to fit the FA, it should provide students with suggestions to improve their level of learning, i.e., to push them toward their learning targets.

Formative Assessment in the EAP Context

Following my Master of Arts research project, which resulted in creating a FA booklet for listening and reading skills for general English classes, I decided to search for sample FA tasks for academic purposes to use in my pre-sessional classes for the reading and writing module. After searching different resources, including commercial EAP books and EAP-related online resources, I noticed that there was a scarcity of FA materials for academic purposes. I therefore decided to review the literature on EAP assessment to see whether FA is in fact practiced in this area of TESOL.

Based on my review, it appeared that assessing students' performance on a pre-sessional course does not follow a common approach in the UK (Banerjee & Wall, 2006). While some universities use commercial tests such as the International English Language Testing System (IELTS), others are reported to use in-house tests. According to the same survey, although some institutions prefer to use in-course performance to assess their students' achievement, most tend to use tests completed toward the end of a course. Most institutions are also required to provide individual reports to either the receiving department or admission office. One recent development in the EAP assessment has been the use of "can do" scales, including lists of performance objectives that EAP tutors can use for the end-of-course reports. These methods of assessment, however, seem to be mainly teacher centered and summative.

The Formative Assessment Project

Together with my graduate supervisor, who is also an EAP tutor, we decided to investigate the effectiveness of formative assessment tasks for monitoring students' learning progress in our reading and writing lessons in a summer pre-sessional course in England. Our students (N=34), who were at a B2 level (IETLS 5.5–6.5) according to the Common European Framework of Reference (CEFR[1]) after two classes, helped us in this project by giving us their perceptions about the effectiveness of using these tasks by completing open-ended questionnaires and interviews at the end of the course.

We developed our FA model based on Heritage's formative loop model (2010). According to this model, FA is considered as an iterative practice with four stages. In our case, these stages represented different parts of the course (almost every two weeks) in which particular teaching and learning activities were completed to close any identified learning gap and ultimately achieve learning objectives set for the course.

Stage one included clarifying which learning objectives we could use as measuring constructs for our FA tasks. We therefore reviewed our course syllabus and created a summary of sub-skills. As the pre-sessional course commenced, we asked our students to complete a needs analysis task, the results of which were also used to fine-tune the syllabus.

From the final list of objectives, we created our first set of FA tasks. These tasks were introduced as we approached week two of our six-week course. The objective was to identify any learning gaps that required feedback, either as a class, in small groups, or individually. Teaching materials and content were also adapted accordingly. We continued the cycle by introducing new learning objectives from the syllabus using a similar sequence. We developed five types of FA tasks for both reading and writing skills. These tasks are described in Table 1 below.

Finally, as we were approaching the last stage of the formative assessment loop at the end of the course, we worked with our students to identify learning gaps that needed to be filled after the pre-sessional course, either through self-study or attending EAP-support courses. Feedback we provided to each student's department included this information.

TABLE 1. FA TOOLS USED IN THIS PROJECT

1. Logs	Focusing on the use of certain sub-skills taught each week
2. Progress Sheet	Monitoring progress by focusing on main course objectives every two weeks
3. Learning Reflection	Reflecting on the learning of specific sub-skills covered each week
4. Self-assessment	Collecting information about students' own learning, analysing what it shows about their progress toward their learning goals and planning the next steps in closing any gaps
5. Portfolio	Collecting and filling all FA tasks and their feedback report sheets

---

[1] The Common European Framework of Reference for Languages (CEFR) is an international standard for describing language ability. It is used to describe learners' language skills.

Reflections on the Formative Assessment Project: Student and Teacher Voices

Students' Reflections

After the course, we asked our students what they perceived as the most significant features of the FA they used and whether these tasks helped them in finding their learning gap, monitoring their progress, and setting learning goals. Next, we summarize what they reported.

🎧 I became aware of my strength and areas to improve. 🎧

One of the benefits of using the FA tasks most often mentioned by students was that they enabled them to identify their strengths as well as aspects of reading and writing skills they needed to improve for their academic studies. The reading log (see Appendix A) is designed for students to monitor sub skills such as scanning and skimming. One of the students stated, "I found it [the reading log] useful to help myself see whether I use the reading techniques I learnt." Another student said, "It is very useful to figure out what you have learned and realize what [you] need to improve." This feedback suggests that these tasks enabled them to answer the two key questions in Sadler's FA framework: "Where are you now?" and "Where are you trying to go?"

🎧 I could monitor my progress. 🎧

Another feature our students noticed was that FA tasks helped them to monitor their progress. As an example, one of the students commented, "I can see my progress easily which helps me to know what I have learned and realize what I still need to improve." Similar to the first feature mentioned above, this feature can also help students answer the two key questions in Sadler's framework.

Among responses highlighting the monitoring aspect of the FA tasks, many students also referred to the motivational impact it had on them. As one of them reported, "I think these tasks are very helpful because I can see my progress easily and this encourages me to work more." We believe that gaining a clearer image of their progress can motivate learners.

In addition to motivating them, some students added that the monitoring feature of the FA tasks they used during their course was focused on their learning progress rather than their scores. For example, one student said that, "Before using FA tasks [in their previous learning context], our abilities were evaluated by how many answers we got right in a test, but the FA tasks focus on reading ability itself and how much we have improved certain sub-skills without any particular score." This aspect of the monitoring feature echoes Clarke, who asserts that FA "promotes a learning orientation in our students, rather than a performance orientation" (2005, p. 22).

🎧 Personalised feedback helped me plan for a clear target. 🎧

The next feature of the FA tasks students identified was their ability to develop a clear learning target and plan for it. As an example, the learning reflection tool for writing (see Appendix B) is organized into three sections to help students identify gaps in their learning. One student reflected, "The writing reflection helped me to spot my weaknesses and strength and enabled me to know what I need to improve." This suggests that the FA tasks helped students to find "where they are trying to go."

In addition to finding gaps in their learning, some students added that once those gaps were identified, they could fill them by using the feedback they received from either their teacher or peers. The role of feedback is central in any type of FA. As Crooks (1988, p. 467) suggested, FA tasks provide feedback that "leads to pupils recognizing their next steps and how to take them." Such feedback seems to enable students to answer the third question in Sadler's framework: "How can you get there?"

I felt a sense of ownership.

Being involved in the learning and teaching process was a noticeable feature of FA tasks that many of our students referred to. Adapting the syllabus based on students' needs seemed to give them a sense of ownership and empowerment in their learning process, as one of them noted: "Completing the needs analysis or the reading progress task made me feel I am a part of this course and can talk about what I need to improve." Giving students a sense of responsibility for their own learning, and considering them as autonomous learners, is one fundamental aspect of FA (Clarke, 2005).

The three main features of the FA tasks students identified are among the key features highlighted in formative assessment models. For example, components of FA proposed in Heritage's model (e.g., learning objectives and success criteria, identifying the learning gap, and learning evidence) were among the features students perceived in using the FA tasks. Similarly, the three conditions in Sadler's framework could also be observed in their responses.

Teachers' Reflections

While the use of FA tasks did not require any major change in our teaching practice, we noticed certain features of these tasks and how they affected our instruction.

Gain understanding of student levels. One of the main features of FA tasks we identified was that these tasks enabled us to understand the learning students achieved. We noticed, for example, that while the end-of-course tests only give an overall picture of students' abilities, FA tasks gave us a better understanding of students' level of attainment in either reading or writing skills at different stages of the course. This feature of FA can be related to one of the key components of the FA process, the learning progression, in which identifying the learning gap and the learning evidence are two of the main elements.

Share learning objectives and expectations with students. Another feature was that some of these tasks (e.g., the needs analysis task) helped us to give our students a clearer picture of what we would cover in the course and what they were expected to learn. This aspect of the FA tasks can also be related to the learning progression element of FA tasks in Heritage's model, in which learning objectives and success criteria are two major components. Sharing learning objectives with students at the beginning of the course and involving them in adapting the syllabus also seemed to provide us with an opportunity to adapt our course content according to the students' specific needs.

In addition to the feedback we received from students through the needs analysis task used at the beginning of the course, the learning evidence received through other FA tasks (e.g., the writing progress sheet) provided us with an opportunity to adjust our teaching to meet emerging student needs during the course. Since summer pre-sessional courses are usually intensive, revising every aspect of the previous lessons is practically impossible, but using the reading and writing progress sheet enabled us and our students to focus more on those areas where they thought they needed further practice.

Give students specific end-of-course feedback on their learning. We also found the FA feedback really helpful for writing a detailed end-of-course report for departments. This enabled us to provide departments with substantial evidence about students' learning achievements as well as needs. Such detailed feedback can ultimately help study advisors guide students towards appropriate language support pathways provided alongside their degree programme.

Don't expect too much too soon. Despite the effective features of FA revealed by this project, we spotted some challenges in implementing these tasks.

One major issue we found was the time needed for checking every individual student's work and providing feedback on those. This can undoubtedly become a problem, especially in large classes. One solution to this problem is to take advantage of peer feedback by dedicating a certain amount of class time to it. Another is to align the course tasks with the FA tasks so that, for example, if students are supposed to read a particular article for a lesson, they can use that same text for their reading FA task.

Another issue was that although many students found these tasks useful, there were some who were dubious about their effectiveness. Some of our students, for instance, found completing FA tasks time consuming and at times too complicated. We realised that it is very important to clarify the purpose of using these tasks at the beginning of the course. Students need to be able to differentiate between the purposes of these tasks compared to typical score-based classroom tests. Unfamiliar FA tasks need to be introduced with care and include some scaffolding to help students understand their purpose.

Conclusion

Assessment in today's educational milieu is shifting from a teacher-centered assessment *of* learning toward a means of enhancing learning through greater learner involvement and effective feedback. Our ultimate message in this chapter is that EAP assessment should involve all participants in a course and be used *for* learning by promoting students' ownership of their learning experience.

....

Saeedeh Haghi is a doctoral candidate and pre-sessional tutor at the University of Warwick.

Dr. Gerard Sharpling is a senior teaching fellow at the University of Warwick.

References

Banerjee, J, & Wall, D. (2006). Assessing and reporting performances on pre-sessional courses: Developing a final assessment procedure. *Journal of English for Academic Purposes, 5*(1), 50–69.

Chappuis, J. (2007). *Seven strategies of assessment for learning: A study guide from Pearson Assessment Training Institute.* Portland, OR: Pearson.

Clarke, S. (2005). *Formative assessment in the secondary classroom.* London, England: Hodder Murray.

Crooks, T. J. (1988). The impact of classroom evaluation practices on students. *Review of Educational Research, 58,* 438–481.

Epstein, M. L., Lazarus, A. D., Calvano, T. B., Matthews, K. A., Hendel, R. A., & Epstein, B. (2002). Immediate feedback assessment technique promotes learning and corrects inaccurate first responses. *The Psychological Record, 52,* 187–201.

Heritage, M. (2010). *Formative assessment: Making it happen in the classroom.* Thousand Oaks, CA: Corwin.

Irons, A. (2008). *Enhancing learning through formative assessment and feedback.* London: Routledge.

Sadler, D. R. (1989). Formative assessment and the design of instructional strategies. *Instructional Science, 18,* 119–144.

William, D., & Black, P. (1996). Meaning and consequences: A basis for distinguishing formative and summative functions of assessment? *British Educational Research Journal, 22*(5), 537–540.

Appendix A

Log Tool

Focus: Reading   **Week 2**

1. Scanning to locate specific information
2. Understanding explicitly stated information

Task	Title	Text type	Comment
1	*Impact of Leadership Style on Organizational Performance: A Case Study of Nigerian Banks*	*JA*	*I could locate the explicitly stated information such as numbers and percentages* *I tried to guess the meaning of some words in the text, but I had to check the dictionary for technical terminology*
2	*10 of the Best Known Leadership Theories*	*JA*	*I used the scanning technique to locate information about each leadership style*
3	*Managing People*	*JA*	*I scanned the text to find the answer to the questions*
4	*NA*	*NA*	*NA*

A. Complete the sentences below based on the articles you were given to read this week.

The text that I found easiest to understand was......*text 3*........because...*it did not have many technical terminology and I could guess the meaning of unknown words.*

The hardest text that I found to understand was *text 1* because *it was very technical and there was a lot of information such as numbers and percentages. It was also very long.*

Instruction:

➢ Keep this Reading log in your portfolio.
➢ Fill the Reading log for every four tasks you do with a certain focus.
➢ For title use the topic of the text.
➢ The first text type is an article from an academic journal
➢ Your comments can be about using the two strategies we learnt this week as well as any other ones you used to understand the text, how easy or difficult you found this type of text or this topic.

B. Compare your reading log with your partner and list any reading strategies you found useful in comprehending the texts.
......*scanning*..........................
............*checking the dictionary*......
............*scanning longer text to only detail read those parts which I need to know about*.....
............*read the headings of the article to choose the parts you need to read in details*.......

Appendix B

Learning Reflection Tool

Focus: Writing/Avoiding Plagiarism   **Week 3**

A.   Tick what you have learnt from last week's lesson and know how to use it/them in your writing.

Topics from last week	What I learnt and can use	What needs improvement	Plan for improvement
1. Using in text referencing and direct quotation to avoid plagiarism	√		
2. Using end of text referencing and indirect quotation to avoid plagiarism	√		
3. Knowing the difference between 'Reporting Verb' groups and using them in indirect quotations	√		
4. Changing sentence structure as a paraphrasing technique		√	• *Familiarizing myself with different sentence structures* • *Completing activities on page 30 of the writing booklet*
5. Changing word form as a paraphrasing technique		√	• *Using the word form table*

B.   Now tick those aspects you still need to improve. Then try to add a brief plan for what you need to do to improve it.

C.   Check your list from part B with your group members and see whether they can also offer any plan for improving the item(s) which need improvement. You can also make suggestions on their list.

D.   If there are any point(s) which need improvement and are the same in your list and other group members', please list their number here.

....................4..............

....

....

....

....

SECTION 2:
VOICES FROM LANGUAGE AND CULTURE CLASSROOMS

6 Our Stories: Narratives for Culturally Responsive ESL Teaching

DEBI KHASNABIS, COERT AMBROSINO, SAINA SAJJADI,
AND CATHERINE REISCHL

It was during the five years I spent as an elementary school teacher that I began reflecting upon the irony that I, the daughter of Indian immigrants, had chosen Spanish as the language to integrate into my professional life. From 1988, when I was first given the name 'Deborita' in my seventh-grade Spanish class, to my early career as an ESL teacher in Southwest Detroit, and finally in my role as faculty for an ESL teacher preparation program, my ability to communicate in Spanish was a source of pride and confidence.

But during my youth, I did not feel the same pride in my own native language. Speaking in Bengali—a song-like language that had the staying power to traverse countries in Asia to counties in southeast Michigan—left me anxious about every word I uttered. In sharp contrast, speaking in Spanish with my adolescent American peers or later with my 4th grade Mexican students inspired me. And strangely, 'Deborita' felt sweet and fun. But it wasn't until adulthood that I proudly asserted the correct pronunciation for my lovingly anointed family name—a name that connotes strength, wisdom and beauty of *the* Hindu goddess: 'Debi–*not* Debbie.'

Over time, I realized that my comfort with Spanish and Spanish-speaking communities was rooted in my borderlands (Anzaldúa, 1987) experience. Having negotiated hybrid spaces between American and Indian worlds and languages, the Spanish language offered me a distinct place of my own—a place that was neither my far off homeland of India nor my family's adopted homeland of America. This recognition of my own story helped me to notice the nuances in the experiences of my elementary school students, and ultimately to engage with them with greater sensitivity. Like me, my students were learning to negotiate life in the borderlands in ways that could be both difficult and beautiful.

Now, as a teacher-educator, I continue to be motivated and informed by this connection between the stories of teachers and their students. I have seen repeatedly that when teachers engage with their own stories, they also engage more deeply with the stories of their students—and ultimately teach with greater sensitivity, compassion, and impact. Having examined my own cultural narrative, I create opportunities for pre-service teachers to analyze and write their own cultural autobiographies before they embark on the sensitive work of English teaching. 🙶 (Debi in 2015)

The coauthors of this chapter teach together at the Ann Arbor Summer ESL Academy (henceforth SESLA) for fourth- through eighth-grade English-language learners (ELLs). SESLA is a U.S. government Title III–funded program that is supported by a partnership between the University of Michigan School of Education and the Ann Arbor Public Schools. Khasnabis and Reischl are SESLA coordinators and faculty at the University of Michigan, and Ambrosino and Sajjadi are teachers in the program and former students in Debi's graduate course in ESL teacher preparation. With a team of other English as a Second Language teachers, we teach a special curriculum every summer that seeks to honor and support the complex language and cultural work that teachers and students engage in as they grow and change together.

In this chapter, we describe the ways that teachers' and students' stories about themselves can serve as resources for teachers who teach using culturally responsive pedagogies. As educational anthropologist Margaret Eisenhart (1995) put it,

. . . telling stories of self is not only a way to demonstrate membership in a group or to claim an identity within it. Telling stories about self is also a means of becoming; a means by which an individual helps to shape and project identities in social and cultural spaces; and a way of thinking about learning that requires the individual to be active, as well as socially and culturally responsive. (p. 19)

Below, we frame four research-based principles for culturally responsive, project-based (CRPB) curriculum that form the core of the SESLA program. Then, drawing on these principles, Saina and Coert illustrate how their stories of self have created pathways for them to understand and connect with their own students' experiences. We contend that having had the venues to represent and share their stories in academic settings, Saina and Coert were inspired and equipped to do the same brave work with their students.

Principles for a Culturally Responsive, Project-Based Curriculum

The SESLA program is designed to be a context in which both teachers and their students generate and draw on their stories of self as they engage in rigorous academic and social learning. The curriculum is rooted in highly interactive thematic instruction that is based on the following core principles:

Principle 1: Draw on Community Resources. ESL teachers learn to perceive community cultural wealth (Yosso, 2005) and to design literacy instruction that recognizes and builds upon community-based knowledge (Purcell-Gates, 2013).

Principle 2: Integrate Multi-Genre Texts and Purposeful Writing. ESL teachers engage students in reading and writing in multiple genres and with authentic purpose in students' lives (Duke, Caughlan, Juzwik, & Martin, 2012).

Principle 3: Create Opportunities for Rigorous and Meaningful Academic Learning. ESL teachers teach the linguistic patterns found in a range of genres, helping students understand language used in school settings to engage with academic content (Bunch, 2006; Filmore & Snow, 2000; Schleppegrell, 2004).

Principle 4: Engage Students in High-Quality Experiences With Multimodal Literacies. ESL teachers use a broad range of media, technology, and symbol systems to integrate reading, writing, listening, speaking, viewing and ways of representing that assist students in their exploration and expression of identities, improvement of academic learning, development of critical literacy and perspectives, and connection of in- and out-of-school knowledge and experiences (Yi, 2014). With these curricular principles in mind, we offer reflections from Saina and Coert about how examining their own cultural stories has equipped them to plan and teach a culturally-responsive, project-based curricula.

Saina's Story

❝ My father was a stranger to me for the first six years of my life. Years would go by when I didn't see him. I remember feeling hurt that I did not have a father. I also remember holding my head up high, and feeling extremely proud that my father was in America, and that one day soon my mother and I would finally leave Iran to join him. The attention and approval I received because I would one day live in America made my father's absence not only bearable but almost worth it. I remember hearing . . . America was 'better.' My connection to America made me feel as though I was 'better' in some way too. I didn't recognize it then but the 'shadow of colonialism,' described by Vandrick (2002), influenced those around me and had influenced me as well. My association with America . . . gave me my first taste of what I recognize now as privilege. But, ironically, my move to America ultimately gave me more than enough tastes of being on the other side of privilege. ❞ (Saina in 2011)

When I wrote my cultural autobiography, I began to realize the value of my experiences. My lack of English-language proficiency had a crippling social and academic effect on me as a new-comer to the United States. I believed others viewed me as someone who had nothing to offer and everything to gain. At school, I was ignored, except for a few instances in the day when teachers or peers would speak to me in extremely loud voices. I never felt integral to the learning community or that I was a source of knowledge. Writing a cultural autobiography allowed me to reflect on my path to becoming an ESL teacher, and to understand the kind of teacher I needed to be in order to be effective.

Every year as our team designs the summer curriculum for SESLA, our goal is to recognize our students, their families, and their communities as sources of unique and profound knowledge (Principle 1). We work to create an environment in which students feel valued and safe. Such an approach would have made my own academic life as a young ESL student a lot more fulfilling.

For example, several years ago, we created an arts-focused CRPB writing curriculum and partnered with a local museum to engage students in interpreting and writing about global artwork, often including pieces of art from the students' home countries. Students later built upon their new knowledge about global artwork to create and write about artistic masks that represented their individual identities.

We visited the museum multiple times, and students ultimately chose an art piece that they felt a connection with. They later wrote an informational brochure that, illustrating CRPB Principle 2, served the authentic purpose of supporting a tour of the museum they would give to their families. The brochures were used during the tour to introduce the piece, explain their connection to it, and to reflect on what they believed the artist's choices symbolized.

These experiences helped students to decide how they wanted to show their identity to others. With the use of several different graphic organizers and activities, students reflected on memories, experiences, and cultural aspects of their lives. They then incorporated their ideas into the creation of their own art pieces, masks that were intended to represent their identities. These activities promoted students' abilities to see themselves, their communities, and their experiences as resources.

I offer the story of a fourth grade student, Javier, to illustrate the experience of CRPB teaching and learning. One morning, Javier sat somberly in front of a mask cut into a unique shape that he explained was the shape of Mexico. He had a soccer ball drawn on the mask, but other than that, it was bare. The withdrawn look in his eyes reminded me of myself as a young ESL student when I felt like I had nothing to offer that would be of interest to others. However, I saw Javier as rich with potential and filled with knowledge. I asked if he had memories of Mexico. He explained that after crossing the border, he had never been back. He seemed to sense my interest and continued to share how his family had travelled to the United States on foot. I expressed my awe of his family's strength and commitment and provided gentle encouragement.

By the end of our conversation, Javier openly described his memories, both painful and powerful. As I walked away, Javier began drawing on his mask with renewed vigor. Later, he confidently presented his piece: "I drew a path from Mexico's flag to the United States' flag. It symbolizes how my family came to America."

It is because I can relate to the trauma of departing one's homeland and arriving in a new land that I understood Javier's experience well. It is this recognition that allows me to fully see my students for who they are and to seize the opportunities I have to honor their life stories. The CRPB principles guided my work in acknowledging students' community-based knowledge (Principle 1) and in integrating purpose-driven products (Principle 2), thus allowing my students to learn English in meaningful ways.

Coert's Story

❝ By opening up about my own life and being honest about my own complexities and inner-conflicts, I believe that I can establish a classroom context in which students feel comfortable to do the same. Not only do I hope that my classroom will be a place where students feel both a sense of belonging and pride in their individuality, but also a setting where they can explore and reflect on ways they feel connected to and different from their familial and community identities. ❞ (Coert in 2012)

As an ESL teacher, I feel it is my responsibility to honor my students' histories without limiting their possibilities. This belief was evident in my autobiography, where I'd discussed my belief that throughout our varied and complex worlds, people strive to both *fit in* and *stand out*. For example, while my Midwestern U.S. upbringing in a white, middle-class household represents an essential part of my identity, this neatly-packaged description could never capture all of the complexities that make me who I am.

All of my life, I have been a lover of language learning. Babbling and beat boxing, I was a child who constantly played with the music and meaning of words. Later, this passion led me to hip hop and spoken word poetry. As I explored these art forms through workshops and competitions in high school, college, and beyond, I began to recognize their potency for creating connections between people from diverse backgrounds.

Meanwhile, I was also delving into second-language learning, discovering a similar hunger to develop my Spanish abilities. I took university courses, studied in other countries, traveled, and later used Spanish in ESL teaching. These are the types of experiences that have enriched and expanded my identity. I carry these perspectives with me as I strive to enact culturally responsive and academically rigorous instruction that integrates multiple genres and literacy modalities in new and interesting ways.

Accordingly, in the 2015 SESLA program, we developed an ESL curriculum that focused on reading, writing, and representing stories of self through the mediums of hip hop, poetry, and video. This design afforded students rich opportunities to practice receptive and productive

English-language skills in their work across these various genres (Principle 4). As students analyzed and discussed exemplar pieces, and later drafted and performed their own work, they practiced the social and academic language that each distinctive genre required. This multimodal approach also provided the context for rigorous and meaningful academic learning (Principal 3), such as instruction around literary devices like metaphor, personification, and onomatopoeia.

Alongside the academic components that undergirded the curriculum, we were also purposeful in the way that we allowed for student choice in the development of their genre projects. We exposed students to stories that strongly demonstrated a connection to their home countries and that represented minority experiences outside of the dominant U.S. culture (e.g., immigration stories). At the same time, we resisted the temptation to "pigeon-hole" students into choosing stories that explicitly related to their cultural heritage. Thus, we also included small moment narratives that someone from any culture could relate to, such as losing a first tooth.

This programmatic design decision was affirmed by my work with Fernando, a Mexican-American seventh grader who wrote a poem about ordering tacos with his mother in a local Mexican restaurant. When I conferred with Fernando during a writing lesson, he explained that he had felt uncomfortable ordering in Spanish in front of his mother and admitted a sense of shame about his home language abilities becoming weaker as he grew up in the United States. Although Fernando was able to explore and discuss these feelings as he revised his poem, he ultimately excluded them from his final draft, deciding instead to publish a celebratory piece that utilized imagery, alliteration, and simile—writing skills we had explicitly studied.

My recognition of the tension I felt as an adolescent to fit in but also to stand out helped me to recognize and honor the duality in Fernando's experience. In that instant, Fernando was fearful about becoming detached from his home culture and his mother, but he also savored the memory of a special moment with her. I know that my students have complex experiences that are neither black nor white but rather various shades of gray, so I believe that they should be encouraged to tell their own stories in whatever way they see fit. In doing so, students are able to explore their own identities and take ownership of the narratives that frame their lives. In the end, sometimes a taco is just a taco, and it was Fernando's right to decide how to tell his own unique story.

In my work with Fernando, stories of self were deeply central to learning. The CRPB principles guided my ability to support him in telling his story in a medium of his choice (Principle 4) and in using writing skills that would promote his continued academic development (Principle 3).

Designing a Curriculum That Draws Upon Teacher and Student Stories of Self

The stories we have shared illustrate the diverse cultural knowledge bases that ESL teachers and EL students have. Like other TESOL scholars researching teacher identity (see, for example, Motha, 2006; Spack, 2006; Vandrick, 2002), we believe that ESL educators often have salient life experiences that draw them to the field. Here we have seen that Debi, Saina, and Coert had enormously different life experiences, but each brought with him or her an understanding of the unique tensions or insights that ESL students may have.

When educators and learners engage in conversation about powerful life experiences, they have the opportunity to make connections based on their diverse life experiences. This is what allows Coert to see a glimpse of familiarity in the experience of Fernando, or Saina to feel kinship and understanding for Javier. It is within these engaging, close-knit settings that powerful learning can take place. A culturally responsive, project-based framework for ESL teaching offers a set of guiding principles that honors both students' and teachers' stories of self while creating compelling contexts for language learning.

Debi Khasnabis is a clinical assistant professor at the University of Michigan School of Education.

Coert Ambrosino is an elementary school teacher in the Adams County School District 14 in Commerce City, Colorado.

Saina Sajjadi is a middle school teacher in the Ann Arbor Public Schools in Ann Arbor, Michigan.

Catherine H. Reischl is a clinical associate professor at the University of Michigan School of Education.

ACKNOWLEDGEMENTS

The authors thank their collaborators in the Ann Arbor Public Schools, Mitchell Scarlett Teaching and Learning Collaborative, and the University of Michigan ELMAC program. We also thank the SESLA students and families.

References

Anzaldúa, G. E. (1987). *Borderlands/la frontera: The new mestiza.* San Francisco, CA: Aunt Lute Books.

Bunch, G. C. (2006). "Academic English" in the 7th grade: Broadening the lens, expanding access. *Journal of English for Academic Purposes, 5*(4), 284–301. doi:10.1016/j.jeap.2006.08.007

Duke, N. K., Caughlan, S., Juzwik, M. M., & Martin, N. M. (2012). *Reading and writing genre with purpose in K–8 classrooms.* Portsmouth, NH: Heinemann.

Eisenhart, M. (1995). The fax, the jazz player, and the self-story teller: How *do* people organize culture? *Anthropology and Education Quarterly, 26*(1), 3–26.

Filmore, L. W., & Snow, C. (2000). *What teachers need to know about language.* ERIC Clearinghouse on Languages and Linguistics. (ED 444379)

Motha, S. (2006). Racializing TESOL teacher identities in U.S. K–12 public schools. *TESOL Quarterly, 40*(3), 495–518.

Purcell-Gates, V. (2013). Literacy worlds of children of migrant farmworker communities: Participating in a migrant Head Start program. *Research in the Teaching of English, 48*(1), 68–97.

Schleppegrell, M. (2004). *The language of schooling: A functional linguistics perspective.* Mahwah, NJ: Erlbaum.

Spack, R. (2006). English lessons. *TESOL Quarterly, 40*(30), 595–603.

Vandrick, S. (2002). ESL and the colonial legacy: A teacher faces her 'missionary kid' past. In V. Zamel & R. Spack (Eds.), *Enriching ESOL pedagogy: Readings and activities for engagement, reflection and inquiry* (pp. 411–422). Mahwah, NJ: Erlbaum.

Yi, Y. (2014). Possibilities and challenges of multimodal literacy practices in teaching and learning English as an additional language. *Language and Linguistics Compass, 8*(4), 158–169. doi:10.1111/lnc3.12076

Yosso, T. (2005). Whose culture has capital? A critical race theory discussion of community cultural wealth. *Race, Ethnicity, and Education, 8*(1), 69–91. doi:10.1080/13613320 52000341006

CHAPTER 7

Sharing Experiences of Intercultural Education Through Student Autoethnographies

GREGORY STRONG

❝ As many Japanese elementary classes do, we had a *kokuban-gakari*, a student in charge of cleaning up the blackboard after lessons, and a *gourei-gakari*, the student who says 'Stand up,' 'Attention,' 'Bow,' and 'Sit down,' at the beginning of the lessons. Our teacher said, 'We come to give a lesson, so you students have to show respect by greeting, bowing, and cleaning up the blackboard before we start.' ❞ (Megumi Homma)

Third- and fourth-year university students like Megumi write an autoethnography in my elective course in intercultural communication in the English department of a Japanese university. In qualitative research, autoethnography is a new and controversial methodology in which a researcher reflects upon personal experiences and relates them to theoretical principles. It offers new perspectives in a broad range of disciplines, including communications and cultural studies. Ellis, Adams, and Bochner (2011) describe it as both method and product because it combines aspects of autobiography with ethnography. Researchers make selective observations about "being part of a culture" and possibly also "possessing a particular cultural identity."

Among the criticisms of autoethnograpy are its lack of a specific methodological approach, its weak validity and reliability, and that its results offer no generalizability. However, these critics suggest rigorous observation, including triangulation of data, using other texts and media. They contend that validity can be achieved by examining the credibility of the narrator and reliability by the verisimilitude of the description. Finally, instead of the traditional notion of generalizability, they substitute the reader's response to an autoethnography: "Does it speak to them?"

My interest in autoethnography is using it as an educational tool that enhances the learning community in my classroom, where we learn from each other as well as from the course readings and my lectures. As with Megumi's observation of the social construct of *power distance*, my students learn to describe cultural value differences in teaching and learning through reviewing their experiences and writing short autoethnographies. Many of my 25 students have been educated abroad for part of their elementary or high school years, or have taken a summer English-language program in another country. The Japanese students without overseas experience have had university classes taught by foreign teachers, and have therefore encountered different cultural values in education.

The class often includes the additional perspectives of international exchange students as well. This year, one Chinese student described her experience with the social construct of *collectivism*:

> ❝ When I graduated from junior high school in northern China, I experienced a 'big event' called Military Training. We trained for one week in the summer, every student, even women like me. Normally four to six people shared a room, but in my case, I had to share one big exercise room with about 80 people. We had to wear green camouflage t-shirts and stand with our hands at our sides and our heels together. We stood like that for 10 to 20 minutes in the heat. If one of us moved a finger the whole group had to stand for even longer. What is more, anything we did had to be done with at least one partner. Even when I wanted to go to the toilet, I had to find someone else to go with me. ❞ (Lianhua Jin)

Theoretical Framework

To help my students create their autoethnographies, I use the framework of Geert Hofstede's cultural dimension theory (1991), which categorizes the impact of culture on a country through a series of social constructs. Easily taught, these constructs help the students reflect on their experiences.

Hofstede developed his theory in the 1970s through his work as a corporate psychologist. He gained access to a large survey database of people working around the world for IBM, and their responses formed a database of some 100,000 questionnaires (Hofstede, 2013, p. 22). He factored the data to formulate the social constructs of *power distance* and *uncertainty avoidance* as well as binary opposites such as *individualism* versus *collectivism* and *masculine* versus *feminine*. Although he would later create additional constructs, he applied these six to education (1986). Skow and Stephan (2000) created a table describing these constructs for a communications textbook.

Hofstede defines these social constructs in educational environments in the following ways. *Power distance* refers to the relationship between students and teachers and the degree of student power. *Uncertainty avoidance* measures the discomfort that students and teachers feel with ambiguity: for example, whether or not students understand that their teacher may not have all of the answers. Hofstede describes *individualism* as occurring, in part, in a society where "one is never too old to learn," while a *collectivist* society believes that education is best undertaken at a certain age, i.e., the "young should learn" (see Table 1). *Masculinity* describes the relative assertiveness and competitiveness in one society, while *femininity* in another expresses cooperation and nurturing. Hiroshi, a student who spent his junior high school years in Fiji, described *masculinity* in his autoethnography.

> ❝ Growing up in Fiji and then moving to Japan made me realize how different cultures impact the way teachers and students interact in school. There, students are encouraged to compete with each other to stand out from the pack. Your score on a test is not as important as where you place in a class of about 30. The top three students are given certificates and rewards such as stationery. Schools have a student council system where 'prefects' chosen by the teachers are on a level higher than everyone else. They can come late to class because they are doing errands for the teachers. It is also very unlikely that a male student would take a subject like home economics because he would surely be ridiculed by his male friends. ❞ (Hiroshi Kizawa)

TABLE 1. VALUE DIFFERENCES IN TEACHING AND LEARNING

COLLECTIVISTIC SOCIETIES: (ARAB COUNTRIES, AFRICAN, MEXICO, PORTUGAL, TAIWAN, JAPAN	INDIVIDUALISTIC SOCIETIES: (GREAT BRITAIN, UNITED STATES, GERMANY, SPAIN, FRANCE)
• Young should learn; adults cannot accept student role. • Students will speak out only when called upon teacher; harmony in learning situations should be maintained at all times. • Education is a way of gaining prestige, getting into higher social class. • Teachers expected to give preferential treatment to some students.	• One is never too old to learn. • Individual students will speak up in response to general invitation of teacher. • Education is way of improving economic worth and self-respect based on ability and competence. • Teachers expected to be strictly impartial.
SMALL POWER DISTANCE SOCIETIES (COSTA RICA, SWEDEN, UNITED STATES, AUSTRALIA, CANADA, NETHERLANDS)	**LARGE POWER DISTANCE SOCIETIES (FRANCE, SOUTH AFRICA, AFRICAN COUNTRIES, ARAB COUNTRIES, JAPAN, KOREA, THAILAND)**
• Teachers should respect independence of students. • Student-centered education. • Teachers expect students to find their own paths. • Students allowed to contradict teacher. • Effectiveness of learning related to amount of two-way communications in class. • Outside class, teachers are treated as equals.	• Teacher merits the respect of students. • Teacher-centered education. • Students expect teacher to outline paths to follow. • Teacher is never contradicted. • Effectiveness of learning related to excellence of the teacher. • Respect for teachers shown outside of class; they maintain authority.
WEAK UNCERTAINTY AVOIDANCE SOCIETIES (CANADA, HONG KONG, INDIA, SWEDEN, PHILIPPINES)	**STRONG UNCERTAINTY AVOIDANCE SOCIETIES (JAPAN, GREECE, PERU, KOREA, AUSTRIA, ECUADOR)**
• Students feel comfortable in unstructured learning situations. • Teachers are allowed to say "I don't know." • Good teachers use plain language. • Students rewarded for innovative approaches to problem solving.	• Students feel comfortable in structured learning situations (precise objective, detailed assignments, strict timetables). • Teachers expected to have all the answers. • Good teacher uses academic language. • Students rewarded for accuracy in problem solving.
FEMININE SOCIETIES (SWEDEN, DENMARK, COSTA RICA, CHILE, SPAIN, FRANCE, FINLAND)	**MASCULINE SOCIETIES (JAMAICA, AUSTRIA, MEXICO, JAPAN, IRELAND, U.S., AUSTRALIA, VENEZUELA)**
• Teachers avoid openly praising students. • Teachers use average student as the norm. • System rewards students' social adaptation. • Students admire friendliness in teachers. • Students try to behave modestly. • Male students may choose traditionally feminine subjects.	• Teachers openly praise good students. • Teachers use best students as the norm. • System rewards students' academic performance. • Students admire brilliance in teachers. • Students try to make themselves visible. • Male students avoid traditional feminine academic subjects.

Sources: L. Skow & L. Stephan, 2000, p. 358; G. Hofstede, 1986.

The Task

Introducing Autoethnography

I begin the student autoethnography task by illustrating the different constructs with scenes from popular films. An episode from the long-running Japanese TV program *9B* illustrates *collectivism*. In a heartfelt speech, veteran teacher Kinpachi Sakamoto reminds his junior high school students that with their classmate, Nao, missing, they are only 29 students, not 30. Class 9B will not be complete until Nao returns.

In the movie *Freedom Writers*, an inspiring high school teacher in Los Angeles, Erin Gruwell, fights violence and racism by developing a student-centered curriculum, thus demonstrating *small power distance*. Gruwell uses her students' journals, which describe their lives, to break down their fears of one another. In a memorable classroom sequence in *Stand and Deliver*, Jaime Escalante, a novice Latino teacher in Los Angeles, compares negative numbers in algebra to digging a hole in a sandy beach, thus using the plain speech of *weak uncertainty avoidance*.

By the second class, the students have a conceptual understanding of the value differences in teaching and learning. At this time, I show them student autoethnographies done by my former students, as well as those on education in Japan, as noted in McDaniel and Katsumata (2011).

Drafting Autoethnographies

Then I lead my students in brainstorming about their experiences with these differences. We have a "free writing" period, during which I circulate among my students, encouraging them as they draft their autoethnographies. I offer writing prompts like "How old were you?," "What was the class?," or "How did you feel at that point?" I also encourage them to use the Japanese terms for specific names or activities. These efforts assist students in creating detailed accounts, such as Rika's description below of *collectivism* while a high school student at an evening "cram school" preparing for her university entrance exams.

> ❝ When I was in cram school, our class was put into a competition with the other classes. We had to get a high enough class average on our test scores in order to beat them. After the project started, we all worked harder, helped each other, and got much closer as a group. Each new test result showed how we had done. When the results weren't good, we sometimes had extra tests or lessons. Even the people who got good grades had to take them. This made us act as one body. ❞ (Rika Wada)

Later in this lesson, each student reads his or her autoethnography to a partner, who then elicits more detail, better approximating the "thick description" of qualitative research. The partner listening asks for people and place names, numbers (such as the number of students in a class), and descriptions of the people and places. The listener takes notes on the first student's replies and later gives them to the writer, who will use them to create more detail in a revision of his autoethnography. The students then switch roles, and take their drafts and notes home to develop 100-word paragraphs for the next class.

Some students will explore two constructs, such as *masculinity* and *collectivism*. Hofstede (1986) describes a masculine culture as one where men are "assertive, ambitious, and competitive" and "respect whatever is big, strong, and fast" (p. 308). This gendered difference, in addition to *collectivism*, is apparent in the following student autoethnography:

> ❝ In my senior high school in Tokyo, we had a huge sports event each Fall. All 16 to 18-year olds, about 900 students, were divided into four teams (red, white, yellow and blue) competing for a trophy. Each of us wore a *hachimaki*, or head band, with our team color. Each team had a *dancho*, a leader, and a *huku-dancho*, or sub-leader, a *shumu*, director, and the only

woman leader, a *zyoseki*, or senior girl. Every day for two weeks, we trained hard after school. We all practiced singing, too, because each team had its own cheer.

The tournament included a soccer game, a tug of war, and a cavalry charge—like a Japanese samurai battle! Teams of riders, with one student standing on the backs of two others, fought with other teams. Each team's riders tried to knock down the other team's riders. When the time was up, the team with the most riders won. Only male students took part, again showing the masculinity in Japanese culture. 🙷 (Miki Tanaka)

In the third lesson, students share their autoethnographies in small groups. They then form new groups and retell their accounts to others. The retelling provides a good opportunity for language development, particularly with longer descriptive accounts.

Even though I have lived in Japan for many years, I find that through this activity, I too learn new things about Japanese culture. For example, as one student reported, in Japanese education, even punishment is often collectively administered:

🙸 In clubs in junior high school, if one person breaks a rule, every club member is punished, too. In my brother's basketball club, the members all had to shave their heads as a punishment. My brother said he didn't mind because everyone had to. But some boys quit instead. In our brass band (I played the euphonium), someone living near the school reported a boy for eating snacks on his way home. He was discovered because our bags have the school name on them, and we have school uniforms and bright purple track suits, too. We were banned from practicing for a week, spending that time, searching our consciences and cleaning the school. All of us had to take *rentai sekinin*, collective responsibility, for his actions. 🙷 (Saki Ueda)

To make the task easier for classes with less language ability, they might be asked to write very short paragraphs for their autoethnographies. Alternately, students could caption personal photos illustrating different constructs, and these captioned photos could be incorporated into a classroom poster session.

The task can be made more challenging by requiring students to write at greater length, perhaps a short essay instead of a long paragraph. A more cognitively demanding task would require students to compare two educational experiences. For example, I asked a graduate student of mine to compare the intercultural differences in *power distance* and *uncertainty avoidance* between her American professor and her Japanese ones.

🙸 In my linguistics class, my American professor often said, 'I don't know,' or even 'some of you may know this area better than me.' Also, he liked to provoke debate among his students, so although we sometimes opposed his ideas, he didn't mind at all. Moreover, he didn't draw conclusions, so we decided for ourselves which points of view sound more plausible. In contrast, I never heard such phrases from my Japanese professors. One professor always boasted about his perfect knowledge in his area and he criticized today's students for their low academic ability. Another professor said, 'I hate to be contradicted, so if you have an opposite opinion, please do not say it in the middle of the class.' 🙷 (Erina Hori)

Student Interpretations of Theory

My students usually develop objections to Hofstede's cultural dimensions theory. His social constructs do not take into account how a country's culture changes over time, the different cultural groups within a nation, institutional and individual differences within a country, and even how national attitudes vary with age and gender.

Before submitting her autoethnography, one student asked me whether she could disagree with Hofstede. By encouraging her, I provided a real-life example of my relatively low teacher *uncertainty avoidance*. It also enabled me to show my class an example of the hedging and qualification that is part of academic discourse. Furthermore, I could introduce the idea of model-building in developing theories and the process by which theories change through objections such as hers.

❝ While an exchange student at a U.S. university, five of my eight classes were very student-centered, with lots of two-way communication, where the teacher brought up students' ideas in class. I had only a few classes like that in Tokyo and that was over several years of university. However, some of my experiences in the U.S. refute Hofstede's work. I never heard a student use a professor's first name, either in or out of the classroom. In class, students were respectful, like, 'Ms. T., would you mind if I open the window?,' and outside class, even between students, they said 'T. gave me a B,' or 'That's Professor A.' One of my male professors even warned us at the end of a lecture of about 100 students against ever using a professor's first name. In contrast, I found younger professors friendlier to students, for example, wearing a Halloween costume, giving us candy in class, or saying 'You can call me Ms. C. or 'Patty' if you want.' Even so, I never heard anyone call her 'Patty.' ❞ (Remi Okazaki)

Scow and Stephan (2000), whose table is included in this chapter, also discuss the limitations of Hofstede's theory, and they suggest that students employ "a critical lens" when discussing its applications to education (p. 359). They note that "The value of models such as Hofstede's lie less in telling us what cultures *are* and more in helping us develop sets of questions about cultures" (p. 359).

Whatever the limitations of Hofstede's theory, it provides a useful framework for my students to create their autoethnographies. Their work helps them to understand complex theories by applying them to their own lives and better understand how cultural and communications theories develop. The task shows them how to look at cultural practices in education from an emic, or insider, perspective as they draw upon their own experiences or while listening to the experiences of their peers. This is a welcome change from other parts of my class in which we study culture through an etic view, the traditional approach of reading and studying descriptions of different cultures. Finally, I have found that listening to each other's experiences builds a stronger sense of community within our class because each of us learns from one another, including me.

....

Gregory Strong is a professor and co-coordinator of the Integrated English Program at Aoyama Gakuin University in Tokyo.

References

DeVito, D. (Producer & Writer). LaGravenese, R. (Director). *Freedom writers*. 2007. [Motion picture]. Los Angeles, CA: Warner Brothers.

Ellis, C., Adams, T. E., & Bochner, A. P. (2011). Autoethnography: An overview. *FQS Forum: Qualitative Social Research Sozial Froschung*, 12(1), Art. 10. Retrieved from http://www.qualitative-research.net/index.php/fqs/article/view/1589/3095#g1

Hofstede, G. (1986). Cultural differences in teaching and learning. *International Journal of Intercultural Relations, 10*, 301–319.

Hofstede, G. (1991). *Cultures and organisations: Software of the mind*. Berkshire, England: McGraw Hill.

Hofstede, G. (2012). Dimensionalizing cultures: The Hofstede Model in context. In L. Samovar, R. Porter, & E. McDaniel (Eds.), *Intercultural communication: A reader* (13th ed., pp. 400–419). Boston, MA: Wadsworth Cengage Learning.

McDaniel, E., & Katsumata, E. (2011). Enculturation of values in the educational setting: Japanese group orientation. In L. Samovar and R. Porter (Eds.), *Intercultural communication: A reader* (12th ed., pp. 365–376). Boston, MA: Wadsworth Cengage Learning.

Menéndez, R., & Musca, T. (Producers). Menendez, R. (Director). Menéndez, R., & Musca, T. (Writers). *Stand and deliver.* (1998). [Motion picture]. Los Angeles, CA: Warner Brothers.

Skow, L., & Stephan, L. (2000). Intercultural communication in the university classroom. In L. Samovar and R. Porter (Eds.), *Intercultural communication: A reader* (9th ed., pp. 355–370). Belmont, CA: Wadsworth.

Yanai, M. (Producer). Kato, S. (Director). (2002). (Broadcast March 7, 2002, video release March 3, 2011). *3 Nen B Gumi.* Nao and Masanori, part III, episode 20, series 6. [Television series]. Tokyo, Japan: Tokyo Broadcasting System.

8 Scaffolding Free Choice in Lessons: Negotiating Global Identity in EFL

EKATERINA TALALAKINA AND IDALIYA GRIGORYEVA

The 10-year age difference between us, the two authors of this chapter, allows us to look at the 21st-century English as a Foreign Language classroom in Russian higher education from two generational and professional perspectives: one of an EFL instructor educated at the turn of the century (Ekaterina) and an EFL student still in the process of acquiring a graduate degree (Idaliya).

In contrast to common student inquiries in the past, which revolved around strictly pragmatic concerns over landing a job by using English as a differential advantage, the students of today gravitate toward a broader axiological spectrum of contemporary global challenges. Thinking beyond purely economic concerns stems from recognizing greater global interconnectedness. Higher education plays a crucial role in fostering an educated stance on current global developments, with the English language as a key variable in attempting to facilitate this process. A fundamental question facing students, instructors, and administrators as major stakeholders in TESOL, therefore, is: "How can we turn an EFL classroom into a platform for building global identity and successfully promoting coexistence in the world community?"

In this chapter, we present a dialogue in which we seek to interpret the positioning of EFL as a platform for global identity, namely through scaffolding free choice of language, soft skills, and ideology.

Great Expectations

Idaliya's View

Having had to compete against 300 applicants for a government-funded spot at the National Research University Higher School of Economics (one of the top 10 in the country), I have experienced the fierce struggle for admission first-hand. Advanced-level proficiency in English as an entrance requirement made me expect that the EFL university curriculum will undeniably take my skills even further, especially given my long-term goal to continue my education abroad.

Ekaterina's View

Indeed, today's students' expectations go way beyond professional needs: Language must also be a tool for success in one's academic, professional, or private life. Many of our students now view it as a tool for making a difference.

But what can we offer them in class if they are no longer interested in traditional grammar, vocabulary, and communicative training, what we studied during our university years? Students like Idaliya view English as a means of exploring world value systems and establishing the place of one's national community in the world arena. This represents a previously unthinkable scenario that is now fostered by global mass and social media.

Like Belcher (2006), we have to consider the evolutionary path of English for Specific/Academic Purposes (ESP/EAP) and take into account not only language use in specific contexts but also the multi-layered nature of such contexts, which extend to communities beyond work and study. This view leads us to the "recognition that learners, as reflective community members, should be empowered to participate in needs assessment alongside ESP professionals" (Belcher, 2006, p. 137).

Confronting Reality

Idaliya's View

Having achieved a comfortable proficiency level upon admission, I shifted my objectives toward a more autonomous approach. I soon discovered that general English is not necessarily enough to meet my academic or professional needs. Exploring all available opportunities for international study or work led me to consider my language, skills, and worldview from a global perspective, raising a number of questions. What regional variation of English should I adhere to? What cultural norms should I consider while practicing such skills as presentations and debate? Which views on content issues are "right"? These questions arose through an emerging awareness of the Russian accent, and others, along with a struggle to adjust to "alien" patterns of text organization and critically review multiple perspectives on sensitive issues.

Ekaterina's View

In response to these concerns, my colleagues and I have applied an integrated approach to designing a Global Debate course. The course was introduced at the National Research University Higher School of Economics in Fall 2014 for 150 undergraduate students during their senior year. Currently taken by 250 students, the course is aimed at reaching advanced, and possibly superior-level, English proficiency. We set this ambitious goal by observing our alumni employed in international organizations like the World Trade Organization, along with statistics showing many of them continuing their education at the world's top universities.

Creating the Global Debate Course

Ekaterina's View

The prototype of the course included several international synchronous and asynchronous projects aimed at a critical discussion of global issues with our American undergraduate counterparts. As discussions continued, however, the idea of an independent institutional debate course within our EFL curriculum took shape. These discussions resulted in general agreement on the benefits of debate courses.

For example, Eckstein and Bartanen (2015) provide a comprehensive overview of the use of British Parliamentary (BP) debate format in undergraduate studies highlighting global citizenship as an outcome of exploring various value frameworks. We agree that the format of debate expands one's cultural perspectives and encourages intercultural sensitivity, yet we have opted for multiple debate formats, including but not limited to BP, following Tessier (2009), who argues that "regardless of format, debates encourage students to develop critical skills and become engaged, informed citizens" (p. 151).

At the same time, we also took into consideration the limitations of debate formats outlined by Goodwin (2003) and Omelicheva (2007), including tensions that can arise from competitive communication styles. To tackle these limitations, we have augmented the debate skills with presentation and negotiation skills to strike a balance between controversy and consensus building in communication.

Ultimately, the model that came to life was a theme-based course revolving around six broad and recurring topics detailed in the annual *Outlook on Global Agenda* report by the World Economic Forum. Relevant for all nations, these topics allow for students' active engagement in formulating specific discussion questions and selecting materials accordingly, thus cocreating the syllabus.

Idaliya's View

What I appreciated most about this course is the substantial amount of communicative training in the form of exercises with active vocabulary collectively selected by students, which ensures collaborative learning and peer review, vocabulary topicality, and relevance to our pragmatic needs. Similarly, content sources include authentic reading and listening materials from various platforms.

The most valuable aspect of the Global Debate course, however, is that the primary focus is neither the content nor the language. The key component of the course is the combined skills of presentation, debate, and negotiation, the ultimate goal of which is to promote *freedom of choice in language, skills, and ideology*.

Ekaterina's View

The teachers set out to achieve the above-stated goal through promoting diversity of accents in speech framing, cultures in skills representation, and world views in content discussion through alternating the skills formats. Table 1 illustrates the correlation between themes, meta-skills, and activity formats in the syllabus. Meta-skills break down into components such as functional language, strategies, and culturally-rooted patterns. The pivotal role rests with micro-training of those components in pairs or small groups, including peer review and self-reflection activities.

In Pursuit of Global Identity

Ekaterina's View

The meta-goal of our Global Debate course is to tackle the global identity issue. Arnett (2002) analyzed psychological effects of globalization on adolescents' identity and concluded that young people develop bicultural identities: One stems from the local culture and the other from their relation to the global culture; the latter is referred to as *global identity*, a sense of belonging to, and awareness of, the global culture (p. 777). In higher education TESOL contexts, this definition can include a complex self-positioning in a multicultural, multilingual, and multi-ideological global environment. In an EFL classroom, in particular, the topic of global identity lends itself to discussions of what kind of language, skills, and content are centrally positioned in the university. In a way, such discussions contribute to the debate in the ELT literature about what linguistic and pedagogical models ELT should be based on (e.g., Ciprianová & Vanco, 2010).

TABLE 1. GLOBAL DEBATE COURSE SYLLABUS OUTLINE

THEMES	META-SKILLS	FINAL ACTIVITY FORMATS	EXAMPLES OF ROLE-PLAYS
Environment	negotiation	multi-lateral negotiations	International Climate Change Negotiations between emerging emitters, the US, the EU, the small island states
Geopolitics	debate	multi-lateral debate	A debate between four parties (groups) categorizing the present state of geopolitical affairs as unipolar world, multi-polar world, zero-polar world (chaos).
Welfare	negotiations	negotiations with mediators	Negotiations between a local trade union and an international corporation with the help of mediators
Diversity	debate	multi-participant debate	US Democratic party debate between presidential candidates within the party on immigration
Freedom	debate negotiations	stakeholder meeting (debate & negotiations)	A meeting of the representatives of various stakeholders of a large trading center on security vs privacy with the goal to work out a policy
Education	debate negotiations	stakeholder meeting (debate & negotiations)	A meeting of the representatives of various stakeholders on international educational initiatives in world's deprived areas

Global language identity. Let's take a closer look at the language, soft skills, and content triad of global identity. The first component deals with the variety of English-language classification options. English for native speakers and ESL are automatically excluded by the context. Yet, three more—EFL, English as an International Language (EIL), and English as a Lingua Franca (ELF)—present an intriguing choice. While English *is* a foreign language in Russia, when it comes to global identity, it is no longer foreign, and can be classified as either international or lingua franca. So what is officially called an EFL classroom is, in essence, an EIL or ELF classroom.

There is no consensus among researchers on the difference between the terms EIL and ELF, with conflicting explanations presented on both sides. In particular, Seidlhofer (2004) argues against the term EIL, claiming that it misleads by suggesting that there is only one clearly distinguishable, codified, and unitary variety. In contrast, Sharifian (2009) insists that EIL, in fact, rejects the idea of any particular variety being selected as a *lingua franca* for international communication. Despite this terminological ambiguity, both acronyms stress variations within World English as a means for intercultural communication and their ownership by the global community.

Idaliya's View

I believe the concepts of EIL and ELF answer our inquiry into English-language identity. Judging from my personal and my peers' experiences, ELT curricula in Russia used to heavily rely on British English. Even today, the tradition is maintained by some "old school" instructors who advocate the native speaker accent. In this regard, I really like the metaphor of "Macdonaldization" borrowed by Jenkins (2006), who vividly argues against this tradition:

> Macdonaldization, whether of the British or American variety, to my mind, has no place in English language classrooms of the twenty-first century unless a learner (having examined fully the facts about world Englishes) prefers for some personal reason to aim for an Inner Circle Accent. (p. 36)

Ekaterina's View

In my view, displaying a strong inclination for a certain native speaker variety of English might lead to a loss of identity associated with the local culture and possibly result in the "identity confusion" described by Arnett (2002). To avoid this, the concepts of EIL and ELF come into play, with the central focus on international intelligibility, highlighting the uniting language features rather than alienating ones. Specifically, studies on ELF show that because certain non-impeding errors are perfectly normal in EFL interactions in pronunciation, vocabulary and grammar, the goals in English instruction should include ensuring intelligibility rather than insisting on correctness (Seidlhofer, 2004). Hence, certain language elements are given greater attention, e.g., vowels, consonants, and sentence stress in pronunciation as facilitators of intelligibility, and idiomatic vocabulary as an obstacle to intelligibility.

Idaliya's View

As for Russian English, ELF as a point of reference addresses many of our inquiries on accents. Pronunciation-wise, the notorious Russian English is pretty intelligible. The Russian "rolling r" is not classified, according to ELF, as a major inaccuracy. However, our grammatical choices explained by the negative transfer from the nonfixed word order of Russian might potentially lead to breakdowns in communication. Some vocabulary choices might also mislead the listener if Russian idiomatic expression is literally translated into English given the false assumption that it is internationally intelligible. Thus, for me it came as a revelation that we need to shift our focus from a more obvious but not impeding feature of our Russian accent to less obvious but potentially impeding "danger zones."

Global identity in soft skills. The multitude of communities students belong to reveal that soft skills acquired through English-language learning are culturally-biased. Namely, the skills of presentations and debate primarily introduce us to the Anglo-Saxon traditions in those domains. It is obvious that strictly structured presentations with linear organization are not typical of Russian discourse organization, while the format of debate is also not widely used in Russian sociopolitical life (presumably given our authoritarian heritage). What struck me as odd when engaging with such skills is that the very format of presentations and debate calls for assessment of the cultural approach to structuring one's world view. Instead of letting the discourse lead the speaker in the moment, strict rules require pre-structuring one's thoughts and predetermining one's strategies. This structure puts the speaker in charge of the discourse outcome and thus encourages responsibility and reflection. Achieving a comfortable proportioning of the two approaches was the hardest task throughout the course.

Ekaterina's View

This contradiction brings us back to Belcher's (2006) argument that it is essential to help learners "appropriate English for their own purposes—to accept, resist, and even push back, to glocalize the global, asserting ownership of English in forms useful in users' own communities" (p. 143). Creating a platform for the students to practice various (sometimes conflicting) approaches to soft skills scaffolds their freedom of choice, enabling them to pick the most appropriate option for each particular situation, either within their local environment or a global one. All these options and variations lead to the idea of negotiation as a meta-skill (in its most general meaning), defined not merely as the trading of positions, but "as a moment of self- and co-definition that may be turned to advantage" (West & Olson, 1999, p. 243). Thus, mastering these skills opens the door to interaction and engagement beyond merely expressing differences in debate.

Global identity in ideology. The soft skills of presentation, debate, and negotiation fall under the umbrella of argumentation, which is key to global identity, because it encourages an explorative and critical approach to reality by testing the validity of the multiple views on this reality (Mirza & Perret-Clermont, 2009). Consequently, content selection plays a pivotal role in the ELF classroom. Giving students a voice in global content exploration not only promotes learner autonomy, but also empowers them to take responsibility for the content issues raised. This approach can challenge the dominant media representation of the issue and lay out a spectrum of related facts and opinions for the students to discuss, evaluate, and eventually choose for themselves. It inevitably uncovers controversies and triggers vigorous debates, but it also provides valuable opportunities to see the bigger picture and understand global society in all its complexity and diversity (Kubota, 2014).

In this regard, it was both intriguing and exciting to watch my students encounter the unpopular opinions on the topics and rephrase them in the debates in ways that made them worthy of taking into account. To be honest, finding the freedom of expressing those views did not come instantly. It took several classes to create the environment conducive to a wider ideological spectrum of approaches to controversial subjects.

Beyond Structured Controversy

Idaliya's View

The most valuable learning outcome of the Global Debate course for me is the recognition of "false debates," i.e., situations generally perceived as a dual confrontation but that actually include more than two conflicting stakeholders. The idea that every debate is in essence multi-lateral and not limited to simplistic "pros and cons" takes the notion of structured academic controversy to the level of an active search for hard-to-reach common ground. This became obvious to me during the discussion of the first topic—the environment versus the economy.

We did not look at environmental issues from the popular perspective of "developed versus developing world." Instead, we sought to research the rationale of the four major parties involved: the United States, the EU, emerging CO_2 emitters, and small island states (see Figure 1). We soon discovered that along with the official rhetoric of the representatives of the developed world (frequently contradicting each other in practice), there is also a strong voice of the emerging countries, which do not have a consensus on this issue. Exploring the positions of the major players not only provided us with necessary data for the debate but also exposed a diversity of opinions that were voiced in many Englishes.

Ekaterina's View

It was interesting to see that for some students, the very existence of the small island states' lobby in the global arena came as a surprise. Everyone initially thought that small island states were the weakest players in the game, but, ultimately, they proved to have the strongest arguments to back their plea to the global community to join efforts in mitigating climate change and regulate economic growth in terms of its environmental impact. Yet, the actual simulation of climate change negotiations uncovered more surprises, as Idaliya explains below.

Negotiations Preparation Worksheet

Assignment: Write down words, collocations and phrases that can help you participate in the in-class activity on the topic.

Unit 1: Climate Change Mitigation and Economic Growth

Stake-holders	Emerging Emitters (1)	European Union (2)	United States (3)	Small Island States (4)
Main Objectives	• mitigate air pollution • sustain economic growth • reducing greenhouse gas emission intensity • increasing non-fossil energy source use • improve environmental & human development indicators	• stabilize atmospheric greenhouse gas concentration • set and fulfil binding emission targets • promoting cleaner building, transport, industry • addressing the issue of waste & landfills	• cutting carbon emissions • promoting sustainable energy strategies • household energy saving • equitable growth • promoting circular economy • sustainable agriculture and fossil fuel extraction	• prevent flooding • prevent sea level rise & ice melting • promote sustainable development across the world • preventing dangerous anthropogenic interference with the climate system • sustainable livelihoods for island residents
Actions Taken	• increasing the use of renewable energy sources • expanding hydro-electric projects (China) • reducing coal consumption (China & India) • promotion of nuclear power generation • vehicle taxes (China)	• promoting carbon trade • recycling • sustainable energy generation from renewable sources • cutting back on nuclear power • walkable cities & public transit development • CO₂ emission targets & constraints	• wide-spread recycling • legal framework for carbon capture • investment in emission-reducing projects in developing countries • improving energy efficiency in building, industry & household appliances • cleaner manufacturing	• global forum participation • raising awareness • sustainable fisheries • fair trade agreements & conditions • land purchases in neighboring states (by Kiribati)
Common Ground	• promotion of cleaner energy sources (renewable, non-fossil) • cutting CO₂ emissions • common interest in carbon trade • preventing global warming beyond the 2°C threshold • improving energy efficiency • energy saving in transport (mostly for 1,2,3) (fuel-efficient cars; constraining automobile usage) ⓞ UN conference ⇒ "Durban Platform for Enhanced Action" (SAR, 2011)			

Figure 1. Negotiations worksheet.

Idaliya's View

While preparing for our first-ever negotiations, my fellow students and I felt confident because we were equipped with relevant facts, necessary vocabulary, functional language, and negotiation strategies. However, the negotiations turned into a debate since we were unable to even attempt to reach a consensus. This unexpected initial failure became a good learning experience. We learned the need to search for common ground rather than beginning by highlighting irreconcilable differences in our positions.

Implications for the Future

Ekaterina's View

Ironically, the Global Debate course developed into a venue for overcoming polarization on multiple levels. First, both students and instructors had "native versus non-native speaker' concerns deeply ingrained in our minds. Our focus on EIL and ELF helped create the atmosphere encouraging freedom of expression rather than obsession with sounding native-like. Second, there was concern that soft skills used in debate and negotiation are alien to Russian culture. Encouraging diversity of functional approaches and trying various communication styles within a safe learning environment proved beneficial in coming to terms with local culture and realizing that we do not have to abandon or idolize it in a cross-cultural setting.

Idaliya's View

Finally, looking at the spectrum of opinions and representing them in role-plays empowered us to take an educated stance on issues that we now feel comfortable discussing, given that there is no right or wrong answer. Gradually, the course evolved into a platform for us to explore our own global identity and made us believe that we can have our voices heard in the global conversations outside of our EFL classroom.

....

Ekaterina Talalakina is an associate professor at the National Research University Higher School of Economics in Moscow, Russia.

Idaliya Grigoryeva is a graduate student at the University of British Columbia in Vancouver, Canada.

References

Arnett, J. (2002). The psychology of globalization. *American Psychologist, 57*(10), 774–783.

Belcher, D. (2006). English for specific purposes: Teaching to perceived needs and imagined futures in worlds of work, study, and everyday life. *TESOL Quarterly, 40*(1), 133–156.

Ciprianová, E., & Vanco, M. (2010). English in the age of globalization: Changing ELT models, restructuring relationships. *The Journal of Linguistic and Intercultural Education, 3*, 123–135.

Eckstein, J., & Bartanen, M. (2015). British Parliamentary Debate and the twenty-first-century student. *Communication Studies, 66*(4), 458–473.

Goodwin, J. (2003). Students' perspectives on debate exercises in content area classes. *Communication Education, 52*(2), 157–163.

Jenkins, J. (2006). Global intelligibility and local diversity: Possibility or paradox? In R. Rubdy & M. Saraceri (Eds.), *English in the world: Global rules, global roles* (pp. 32–39). London, England: Continuum.

Kubota, R. (2014). "We must look at both sides"—But a denial of genocide too? Difficult moments on controversial issues in the classroom. *Critical Inquiry in Language Studies, 11*(4), 225–251.

Mirza, N. M., & Perret-Clermont, A. N. (2009). *Argumentation and education.* New York, NY: Springer.

Omelicheva, M. Y. (2007). Resolved: Academic debate should be a part of political science curricula. *Journal of Political Science Education, 3*(2), 161–175.

Seidlhofer, B. (2004). Research perspectives on teaching English as a lingua franca. *Annual review of applied linguistics*, 24, 209–239.

Sharifian, F. (Ed.). (2009). *English as an international language: Perspectives and pedagogical issues* (Vol. 11). Clevedon, England: Multilingual Matters.

Tessier, J. T. (2009). Classroom debate format. *College Teaching*, 57(3), 144–152.

West, T., & Olson, G. A. (1999). Rethinking negotiation in composition studies. *Journal of Advanced Composition*, 19(2), 241–251.

Throwing Away Stereotypes: Deepening Intercultural Understanding Through Cambodia-Japan Letter Exchanges

NICOLE TAKEDA

When I asked a group of Japanese university students to give their impressions of Cambodia, one of the world's poorest countries, their descriptions frequently included adjectives such as "dark," "dirty," "poor," "no education," and "no dreams." My students equated living in poverty with living less of a life than people who live in developed countries like Japan. Although my students attributed these negative images to the media, they did not realize that many of their stereotypes were the result of comparing another culture to their own Japanese cultural norms and values. To address these stereotypes and foster intercultural communication competence, I asked my students to participate in a four-month letter-writing exchange with disadvantaged Cambodian students. After three letter exchanges, my students showed better awareness of their stereotypes as they gained intercultural communication competence. The process also spurred greater interest in their own heritage and helped them form international friendships. In this chapter, I share what my students and I learned from the letter-writing project.

Merging Pen Pal Writing and Intercultural Communication Competence

Pen pal writing between students started in the 1920s after Dewey (1899–1959) recognized that letter writing allows children to fulfill their desire to share their experiences and in turn learn the experiences of others. His belief that language instruction should create a "real desire to communicate vital impressions and convictions" (p. 66) prompted instructors to add letter writing to their curricula. Since then, it has been used for a variety of purposes. Ceprano and Garan (1998) investigated how letter writing helps the development of children's writing skills; Yamada and Moeller (2001) examined how it affected student motivation and second-language acquisition based on national standards.

Another study (Austin, 2000) explored the critical thinking skills of elementary students who corresponded with college students taking a children's literature course. Other projects created opportunities for pre-service teachers to acquire cultural knowledge that helped them teach linguistically and culturally diverse students (McMillon, 2009; Walker-Dalhouse, Sanders, & Dalhouse, 2009).

This chapter echoes the purpose of Barksdale and colleagues' (2007) research, which demonstrated that letter writing can help students develop their understanding of different cultures. It further builds on that cultural understanding to show how these exchanges, as part of cultural content lessons, can address stereotypes and develop intercultural communication competence. This holistic teaching approach is "relevant, meaningful and serves a real purpose," because students can interact and learn from each other (Goodman, 1986).

It is human nature to make generalizations to help understand the world and the people around us; because of this, we tend to create stereotypes, which are overgeneralizations and oversimplifications about the features of a group of people (Barna, 1998). Stereotypes can help guide our general behavior toward this group (Samovar, Porter, & Stefani, 1998), but they ignore individual differences among those group members (Brislin, 1993).

To identify and avoid stereotypes in cultural content, instructors can use pen pal exchanges to promote cultural awareness, which is the ability to understand and explain one's own culture and do the same with another culture (Tomalin & Stempleski, 1993). Cultural awareness enhances intercultural communication competence so that learners have "the ability to acknowledge, respect, tolerate, and integrate cultural differences that exist between individuals, social members, ethnic groups, and countries" (Han, 2013, p. 6).

This broadening of perspective is especially important for Japanese university students, who tend to be narrowly focused on securing employment during their third and fourth years of study. The aging and declining population of Japan will make intercultural communication competence more necessary for my students since Japanese companies see opportunities for growth in markets outside of Japan.

Learning Context

The letter-writing exchange was run between two institutions from 2011 to 2015. One of them was Aoyama Gakuin University (AGU) in Tokyo, Japan, where I work as an English as a Foreign Language and intercultural communication instructor, and the other one was my own non-governmental organization (NGO), the Bayon English Academy (BEA), in Siem Reap, Cambodia. BEA is a nonprofit language school for disadvantaged youth that I started in 2010 to provide English lessons from well-trained, professional Cambodian teachers in modern facilities, a rarity in the country's education system (Takeda, 2015).

On the Japanese side, the students were from the English Literature department, enrolled either in the department's required *Integrated English Core 3* (IE3) course or an elective *Intercultural Communication* (ICC) seminar. The IE3 classes use Task-Based Language Teaching (TBLT) that focuses on discussion skills through student-led discussions and presentations. Students also develop their reading and writing skills with book reports and journal writing. The course was flexible enough that I could substitute the letter-writing exchange project for the journal writing.

The ICC seminar, however, uses content-based instruction (CBI), in which students learn theoretical concepts and apply them to case studies and personal experiences so that they can identify shared cross-cultural values and appreciate the differences. Students met weekly for a three-hour session during a 15-week semester. The academic levels of the students ranged from mid-intermediate to high-advanced, and they included first-year to third-year students. Class sizes ranged from 16 to 25 students. The Japanese students were all new to the letter-writing project.

On the Cambodian side, all learners came from families living in extreme or moderate poverty, making 1 or 2 (U.S.) dollars a day, respectively (Ravallion, Chen, & Sangraula, 2009). They lived in the slums in Trapeang Sess village, which is less than five kilometers from Angkor Wat, the world's largest temple. They attended English lessons at my school from Monday to Friday for one hour a day. A TESOL-trained Cambodian instructor taught using a task-based communicative approach over two semesters in a one-year program, which totaled about 200 hours of classroom instruction.

The school offers four EFL programs, but the students in the letter-writing exchange were enrolled in the *Pre-Intermediate*, the *Intermediate*, or the *Advanced EFL Program*. There was an average of 20 to 24 students in each class, which is less than half the size of their public school classes (Takeda, 2015), and they ranged in age from 13 to 22, with 17 being the average age.

They were also at different stages in their education, with most of them either in high school or recent graduates. Those in public school struggled to remain there because of expensive fees for uniforms, textbooks, and private tutoring. They learned English with the hope of finding a job in the tourist sector because it offers higher salaries than those in agriculture, construction, and market stalls. They can then help their families pay for their school expenses (Takeda, 2015).

In this chapter, I focus on the perspective of the Japanese learners because some Cambodian students had repeatedly participated in the project. Moreover, the Cambodian learners have had much more exposure to different cultures due to the heavy influx of overseas tourists in Siem Reap.

Most importantly, addressing stereotypes and prejudices in Cambodia could become political because prejudice toward the Vietnamese would likely dominate discussions. This is because every single student at my school had a family member who died during the 10-year Vietnamese occupation (1979–1989) to oust the communist Khmer Rouge regime (1975–1979). In addition, the Ministry of Interior could revoke my NGO status for teaching and discussing any type of political content, which the government strictly prohibits, so I must self-censor my school's course content, textbooks, and library books to continue my work there.

Letter Writing Exchange Project

The project had five goals: (1) to develop students' intercultural understanding through learning about their own culture and their partner's culture; (2) to identify and avoid cultural bias, such as stereotypes and prejudices; (3) to compare and contrast Japanese and Cambodian cultures; (4) to develop communication strategies to overcome information gaps and misunderstanding; and (5) to develop a friendship with an English learner from a different culture.

To achieve these goals, students had to write a minimum of three letters on designated topics. For the first topic, students wrote a self-introduction and described their lifestyle. The second was on a cultural practice, and the third described the students' experiences in educational institutions. Students also had to write about recent news in their lives.

When students received their letters in class, they first listened to a 20-minute lecture connected to the letter's theme. After they read them, they reported the content of the letters to their respective groups and discussed it. Next, they shared their letters and discussed two questions about them.

They then broke off into pairs to complete a *Cultural Awareness Activity* and later reported their conclusions to their groups. Their last two tasks were given as homework: One was a reflective writing task about their letter submitted as a blog post on my teaching website; the other was to write their next letter.

In the next lesson, students completed another *Cultural Awareness Activity* based on their previous week's blog postings and reported their opinions to their groups. They then read each other's letters written to their pen pal partners and made suggestions on how to communicate cultural content, such as giving definitions or drawing pictures to explain culture-specific vocabulary.

Figure 1. AGU students with their first letter from their Cambodian partners.

Before I mailed the letters, I read all of them so that I could prepare a cultural knowledge lesson for the Cambodian students. I did the same before the Japanese students got their letters, but for them I focused more on cultural awareness. Larrotta and Serrano (2012) did the same with their participants' letters, but their "mini-lessons" provided students with additional practice on grammatical points.

Discoveries

Impact of Stereotypes

One of most important revelations the Japanese students made during the project was that most of what they knew about Cambodia was based on stereotypes. McMillon's (2009) study also shows that stereotypes were brought to the surface through pen pal exchanges. One common stereotype my students recognized was that their pen pal partners "didn't look poor." They also expressed surprised that "poor students" could communicate in English, play sports, and use the Internet. They also didn't expect their partners to have hopes and dreams because of their economic status: "My partner wants to run a company. Cambodia is a poor country, so I thought it's difficult to have a big dream like that." Learners realized that examples like these were stereotypes by identifying and discussing stereotypes in each other's blog comments about their partners. When students bring their interpretations from their "personal workspaces" to a "shared cognitive workspace" through peer-group discussions, this can "enhance or alter" understandings (Gambrell et al., 2011).

Figure 2. BEA students with their second letter about Japanese cultural practices.

By the last letter, my students had recognized the negative impact of stereotypes on inter-cultural communication. One student admitted: "It is embarrassing to realize my ideas about countries were actually stereotypes. Having them can hurt others and they make it more difficult to get to know each other." Another said, "Throwing away stereotypes is the most important thing in intercultural communication [because] they can give us images of people that can hurt them."

Many students contributed their stereotypes to media coverage of developing countries: "I had stereotypes about poverty and developing countries. . . . I thought no kids could go to school . . . had no food to eat and no job to make money. I am so ashamed of myself because all those ideas [I had] were made by the media." Samovar, Porter, and Stefani (1998) support such claims about the mass media influencing the formation of stereotypes.

Acquiring and Exchanging Culture

The next discovery my students made was about the importance of knowing their own culture. All of the learners had simply considered themselves Japanese without thinking deeply about their culture and values. Like McMillon's (2009) pen pal participants, this project also "challenged them to think about where they came from, and who and what influenced their values and beliefs" (p. 129), and to realize the importance of acquiring and exchanging cultural information. One student wrote, "I have been to other countries, but I feel like I have never explained Japan well. This made me realize that it is important to know my country."

Students also noted that trying to explain Japanese cultural values motivated them to learn more about Japan. As one learner pointed out, "I discovered that I didn't know a lot about my own country. I was ashamed because I had thought that I knew a lot about Japan. I've decided to learn more about Japan." Other pen pal exchanges also cited an impact on motivation for learning about other countries and cultures (Barksdale, Watson, & Park, 2007; Larrotta & Serrano, 2012; McMillon, 2009).

Learning and exchanging cultural information also helped students realize how people from different cultures are connected through similarities. As one student eloquently articulated: "I learned that people are the same. . . . I became aware that we can make friends with those of any age, nationality, and religion if we open our mind. . . . I feel my partner is my sister. I have never met her, but I feel that she is a member of my family." Barksdale, Watson, and Park (2007) reported similar connections between American and Malawian pen pals: "Students express a strong desire for connectedness as they gain an appreciation for both the similarities and distinctions that define their native cultures" (p. 66). The letters and classroom activities allowed the Japanese students to explore their heritage and helped them see they were more similar to than different from their partners, which contributed to developing their intercultural communication competence.

Gaining Cultural Awareness

Finally, Robinson (1985) claims that acquiring cultural awareness is a gradual process. Barksdale, Watson, and Park (2007) report that their pen pal project "promoted the development of conceptual knowledge and cultural understandings" (p. 66) over a three-year period through seven letters. In this exchange, however, students achieved cultural awareness after only three letters over four months. The entire project took only nine hours of class time out of the 45 hours allotted for the course. This accelerated acquisition can be attributed to the variety of classroom tasks that had students listen to mini-lectures while filling in knowledge gaps, complete activities to help them understand their letters more deeply through group work, and do homework assignments to reflect independently on those activities.

Despite the limited time and interactions, the Japanese learners gained an awareness of both cultures and improved their ability to explain them, all of which contributed to the development of their intercultural communication competence. As one student eloquently remarked: "My partner made me realize that happiness does not just come from the accumulation of goods, but from the life you have and the people around you." Another student discovered that ". . . there are so few chances to actually understand [global] problems when living in Japan. I am really glad that I had the chance to realize this. I feel that I know more about world problems, and it is my turn to pass the message onto to people around me."

Figure 3. AGU students reading their letters from their Cambodian partners.

Figure 4. BEA student showing off his letter he wrote for his Japanese partner.

Conclusions

To help students improve their intercultural communication competence, teachers need to be willing to foster candid discussions about race, gender, and socioeconomics. During the project, I had to reassure students that it is natural to have stereotypes so that they would not be ashamed, and reluctant, to share their opinions. Moreover, sharing my own experiences living in different cultures created an atmosphere that helped students feel more comfortable discussing their assumptions about Japan and Cambodia. At the same time, I had to be careful not to judge the Japanese learners for holding negative stereotypes about the Cambodian students. Negative stereotypes also arose when Japanese students questioned my knowledge about Japan simply because I am not Japanese. In both cases, questioning students in a sensitive manner about why they held certain assumptions provided opportunities for learning and growth.

The most rewarding part of this project was that I was able to bring together two groups of students from diverse cultural and socioeconomic backgrounds to help them discover that they were more alike than different. From my experience, other Cambodian NGO students would greatly appreciate the chance to connect with Japanese students. However, project leaders will need to consider costs, logistics, and the school itself. This project was possible because I funded it myself, which included paying for courier services to deliver the letters to and from Cambodia because the postal system there is notoriously unreliable. Undelivered letters would have affected the students' cultural awareness process and created havoc with teaching schedules both at my university and the NGO. In addition, teaching quality, resources, and facilities vary greatly among NGO and public schools (Takeda, 2015), which would make it difficult to replicate this project. This is not to say that similar pen pal projects cannot be done, but teachers will need to be patient, persistent, and flexible when collaborating with schools in developing countries.

Nonetheless, teachers can provide other types of authentic interactions to promote cultural awareness and contribute to intercultural communication competence. They can include field trips, guest speakers, or volunteer opportunities, all of which allow students to interact with people from different cultural and/or different socioeconomic backgrounds. Every single interaction is a chance for them to challenge their own cultural values or even to inspire change among those in their own culture. The Chinese philosopher Lao-tzu once claimed that "a journey of a thousand miles begins with one step" (quoted from Moncur, 2015), but our learners do not have to take a single step outside of their classrooms to travel far on a cultural awareness journey.

....

Nicole Takeda is an adjunct professor at Aoyama Gakuin University in Tokyo.

References

Austin, P. (2000). Literary pen pals: Correspondence about books between university students and elementary students. *Reading Horizons, 40*(4), pp. 273–294.

Barksdale, M. A., Watson, C., & Park, E. S. (2007). Pen pal letter exchanges: Taking first steps toward developing cultural understandings. *The Reading Teaching, 61*(1), 58–68.

Barna, L. M. (1998). Stumbling blocks in intercultural communication. In M. Bennett (Ed.), *Basic concepts of intercultural communication*. Yarmouth, ME: Intercultural Press.

Brislin, R. (1993). *Understanding culture's influence on behavior*. Fort Worth, TX: Hart Brace College Publishers.

Ceprano, M. A., & Garan, E. M. (1998). Emerging voices in a university pen pal project: Layers of discovery in action research. *Reading Research and Instruction, 38*(1), 31–56.

Dewey, J. (1899/1959). *Dewey on education*. New York, NY: Teachers College Press.

Gambrell, L. B., Hughes, E., Calvert, L., Malloy, J. A., & Igo, B. (2011). Authentic reading, writing, and discussion: An exploratory study of a pen pal project. *The Elementary School Journal, 112*(2), 234–258.

Goodman, K. (1986). *What's whole in whole language?* Portsmouth, NH: Heinemann.

Han, Y. (2013). Research on fostering intercultural communication competence on foreign language learners. *Cross-Cultural Communication, 9*(1), 5–12.

Larrotta, L., & Serrano, A. (2012). Pen pal writing: A holistic and socio-cultural approach to adult English literary. *Journal of Adult Education, 41*(1), 8–18.

McMillon, G. M. T. (2009). Pen pals without borders: A cultural exchange of teaching and learning. *Education and Urban Society, 42*(1), 119–135.

Moncur, M. (2015). *The quotations page*. Retrieved from http://www.quotationspage.com/quote/24004.html

Ravallion, M., Chen, S., & Sangraula, P. (2009). Dollar a day revisited. *World Bank Economic Review, 23*(2), 163–184.

Robinson, G. L. (1985). *Cross-cultural understanding and approaches for foreign language: English as a second language and bilingual educators*. Oxford, England: Pergamon.

Samovar, L. A., Porter, R. E., & Stefani, L. (1998). *Communication between cultures*. Belmont, CA: Wadsworth.

Takeda, N. (2015). *Perspectives on teaching English at an NGO in Cambodia*. Alexandria, VA: TESOL Press.

Tomalin, B., & Stempleski, S. (1993). *Cultural awareness*. Oxford, England: Oxford University Press.

Walker-Dalhouse, D., Sanders, V., & Dalhouse, A. D. (2009). A university and middle-school partnership: Pre-service teachers' attitudes toward ELL students. *Literacy Research and Instruction, 48*(4), 337–349.

Yamada, Y., & Moeller, A. J. (2001). Weaving curricular standards into the language classroom: An action research study. *Foreign Language Annals, 34*(1), 26–34.

CHAPTER 10

Pragmatic Development and the Study Abroad Experience: Building and Maintaining Competence

MARK FIRTH, JAMES BROADBRIDGE, AND JOSEPH SIEGEL

Even after 10 years of living in Japan, we still feel a great sense of relief when entering a restaurant and realizing that there is an English menu or one with pictures. Similarly, we are pleased at times when we are asking for something in a store, or when we cannot understand what someone is asking us, that there is someone nearby who speaks English and is ready to step in and help.

These simple, everyday interactions instill in us, as teachers, a real sense of empathy with our students as we send them off on study abroad (SA). Our aim is to enhance their ability to communicate and function effectively while abroad because this ability will influence the quality of their SA experience, including linguistic development.

While SA has been shown to benefit students' linguistic, social, and academic abilities (e.g., Kinginger & Farrell, 2004), their pragmatic competence and understanding of social and linguistic norms (Taguchi, 2015) are also vital. Findings suggest that spoken pragmatic development demands more attention in English as a Foreign Language classrooms (e.g., Ishihara & Cohen, 2010). As teachers and administrators who send a number of students to SA, we feel the need to better understand how we can prepare our students for the SA experience.

This chapter is based on a larger study into Japanese university students' pragmatic development during SA (see Siegel, 2015, for further details). In that study, participants took part in sessions that included language practice to assess their pragmatic speaking ability. Interviews were conducted before, immediately after, and six months after their return from studying in the United States for one semester. Participants in the study were first-year Liberal Arts students at a university in Japan. They had yet to choose their majors, but had enough interest in English to decide to study abroad.

This chapter focuses on two participants who we felt illustrated the varied effects that SA can have on students. We will also examine student motivation and how the output and narratives of these students helped to create a more practical approach to our pre- and post-SA teaching sessions. The sessions incorporate speech acts, self-assessment, and self-reflection in the EFL classroom as an alternative pedagogy for teachers who want to better equip students to function in the target SA community.

Student Achievement After Studying Abroad

As teacher-researchers, we were initially interested in the linguistic improvements our students made while on SA. For the purpose of our study into pragmatic ability, we used oral discourse completion tasks (ODCTs) to assess students' abilities to complete certain speech acts (see Siegel & Broadbridge, 2016, for further details). Table 1 shows the progress made by two students who studied abroad, Tom and Marv (pseudonyms). In their immediate post-SA sessions, we see longer responses, more variety in the grammatical structures used, and greater awareness of pragmatic norms and expectations. We were surprised, however, by the contrast between them six months later. In the final ODCT session, Marv continued to show further signs of improvement, whereas Tom appeared to have regressed to his level prior to studying abroad. We felt we needed a deeper understanding of these differences in linguistic output.

Student Motivation After Completing Study Abroad

During the six months post-SA, Marv continued to be a highly motivated student, taking language classes and maintaining regular contact with friends made while on SA. In contrast, Tom found little opportunity to speak English and, in fact, decided not to continue his English studies. It was perplexing to us how a learner could go overseas, experience the target language and culture in a positive way, yet end up less motivated than prior to departure.

This divergence in motivation levels and progress in learning English so soon after SA suggested to us there might be a need for more support pre- and post-SA, as well as the need for tasks to be carried out whilst students are abroad. Pre-SA sessions, for example, would work on developing pragmatic competencies and negotiating meaning when misunderstandings arise, whereas post-SA sessions would be used for discussing both the positive and the negative experiences each student had while abroad. Finally, we would ask students to explore their future goals for their English language learning specifically and for their lives in general.

Student Interviews

After SA, we video recorded and transcribed student interviews. We asked the students about many aspects of life while abroad and about the support they received before and after SA.

Increased Support Prior to Departure

A number of students noted a strong desire for more contact and opportunities to practice with international students prior to departure. Noticeably, Marv, who made very good progress in his language skills, told us, "I found it useful when I got help by practicing with English teachers before [going abroad]." In the participants' home university, students can participate in English language circles at lunchtime, when they can practice speaking with instructors. To have dedicated sessions for SA students would be difficult to organize, but we now believe that we could assign some lunchtime sessions to focus specifically on improving pragmatic strategies, as opposed to free conversation. Such focused training might help students in their initial interactions with classmates when abroad.

TABLE 1. LONGITUDINAL CHANGES IN STUDENT ORAL DISCOURSE COMPLETION TASK PERFORMANCE

Participant		ODCT	Pre-study abroad response	Post-study abroad response	6 month post-study abroad response
				PROGRAM: 1-SEMESTER STUDY ABROAD SAN FRAN.	
Mary		Apologizing to a friend	I'm sorry I forgot to bring notes, so can you wait for a minute? Uh, I'll bring it.	Oh, I'm sorry. I forgot to bring notes from for the project, so can you make another schedule for me?	I'm sorry Jessica, I forgot to bring some notes for our class project. So they are in the class, so I'll take it and give it to you after, after, after that.
		Giving a compliment	It was great lec ah lecture. I was really excited and enjoy your class. I would like to take your class always.	So, I'm glad to have taken your class, Mr. ah, Professor Smith. If I can, I want to take your another class.	Professor Smith, today's lecture is really great. I'm interested in music more than before. So maybe I'll take, I'd like to take your class again next se in the next semester
		Thanking	I'm sorry because late. Ah, I lost my textbook uh so I if you like I I give you a something special.	So, thank you for lending me this textbook for a long time. Ss, by the way, I bought some some cakes for you, so let's let's eat them.	OK, thank you for lending me lending me your textbook. It helped me a lot. So if you have time, can you, can we eat lunch together? It's on me.
Tom		Apologizing to a friend	Ah, sorry Jessica. I forgot my note in the classroom. Ah, I . . . can I take can I take to the classroom?	Jessica, I forgot my notebook. Ah, I should I should get the notebook right now, so could you wait for a minute? Just just a moment.	I forgot to bring the notes, so I am so sorry. I will go to take it soon, I will be back here soon.
		Giving a compliment	Your presentation was so awesome. I want to get to do like yours. Yes.	That was so good. I never seen like your presentation. Ah, I want to I want to do p-presentation like you and I want to be like you.	It was the great presentation ever for me. oh, I want you to help me do presentation.
		Thanking	Molly, ah, I could, I could finish my homework because of your help. I'll buy you lunch today.	Oh, oh, this is your textbook. Ah, if I if you didn't borrow me your textbook, maybe I would not I would not do my homework, so I appreciate it. Thank you.	This is your textbook. Thank you for helping me. I really appreciate it. Thank you.

This need for a focus on pragmatic speaking strategies was highlighted by another student, Tom, who told us in his interview, "I had to change roommates after three weeks because he was too messy." Through more focused instruction and practice, our aim is to better equip our students to deal with potentially difficult interactions, such as complaining. With more pragmatic ability, Tom might not have had to wait three weeks to change roommates; rather, he could have resolved the issue with his roommate by himself.

Another suggestion volunteered during interviews was for more opportunities to ask questions of teachers prior to departure. Currently, most of our SA programs are organized separately from language classes. This is clearly a missed opportunity for preparing students both linguistically and culturally for their SA. Interestingly, it was Tom who reported that he had a fruitful discussion with his teacher while abroad: "I asked the teacher questions after the class. The teacher invited me to lunch. We talked about life in Japan, my life, my future." Tom went on to explain that teachers could help students find a purpose for studying abroad and help them realize their dreams. He said that the lunchtime question-and-answer session he had in Japan with a teacher was good, but he wanted more.

Most teachers who have taught for a number of years can remember the individual students they have touched or influenced. One of the authors of this chapter recalls, "I clearly remember telling one of the students at her graduation party that she should follow her dream and simply go to Africa for a year if that was her desire. After refusing her job offer, that was what she did. One year later, a very changed young woman came back to Japan and thanked me for helping her find her way in life." Sometimes students just need a little push and encouragement to take the first step. This and similar reflections magnified our belief about the importance of student contact with teachers prior to departure. Student voices and our reflections on them now make our task clear. We will have to make proposals to administrators in order to align our program with the expressed desires of our students.

Student Difficulties While Abroad

Overall, we felt that the interview responses, along with our analysis of the ODCT sessions, highlighted the weaknesses that exist in our current SA programs both before and after going abroad. One of the biggest problems students experienced while on SA was in their interactions with staff in the service industry. Our students reported feeling particularly pressured and nervous. Students mentioned problems related to being mistaken for native speakers and not knowing how to deal with this. Tom said, "I told (explained) I was an exchange student," after which the staff spoke more slowly to him. What we do not know, however, is what Tom actually said to the staff member, how effective and efficient this interaction was, or how this correction was received by Tom's interlocutor.

Marv also reported that he felt frustrated sometimes when talking with people in stores and cafes. Unlike Tom, however, Marv told us that after a while, "I could talk to strangers and ask (them) to say it again when they don't understand me." A greater focus on improving students' pragmatic abilities should aid them in situations such as these and introduce them to strategies to interact with greater confidence. For instance, we now wish we could have given outbound students extra practice in communication strategies such as circumlocution skills and response tactics.

Reforms to our Study Abroad Support

Student output during ODCTs and personal narratives generated through student interviews have helped us to develop a number of recommendations that teachers embarking on creating SA programs should find useful.

Teaching Pragmatic Strategies

We feel the same ODCT situations that we used as part of our research could be expanded and used in dedicated SA classes or drop-in lunchtime sessions. The Appendix displays a small sample of situation cards, which have been expanded to cover the same speech acts, but with differing levels of formality. Students could practice, video-record, and view themselves to gain awareness of their strengths and weaknesses. Teachers, international students, or even post-SA students could also demonstrate effective strategies and language to help students increase their pragmatic knowledge of the norms expected in their host community.

Ideally, we would like to set up pre- and post-SA sessions in which we provide students with immediate linguistic feedback as well as contextual advice for their target cultures. These post-SA sessions should reenact the same scenarios in order to demonstrate student progress. Students would then have a record of their pre-SA and post-SA output and would hopefully be able to see and assess the gains they have made both linguistically and strategically.

Strategies for Motivating our Students

It's important that we address the need for facilitating learners' motivation before, during, and after their experiences abroad. Fryer (2012) identified six strategies for study-abroad learners to facilitate L2 motivation and acquisition. Of these six, we identified two strategies that we would like to incorporate into our SA programs immediately, which can quite easily be attained through the use of notebooks.

The first strategy is using goal setting and visualization in order to assist students in visualizing their L2 selves. In predeparture classes, we will have students write their language goals and describe their ideal future selves. Upon returning from their time abroad, learners will check their notebooks and rewrite these self-images. By identifying the discrepancies between their ideal and current selves, learners will have clearer ideas of their goals and what they need to do to achieve these goals.

The second strategy is providing learners with the skills required to become effective, autonomous learners. Students will be asked to list five or six situations they believe they will find themselves in while abroad. They will then write an appropriate speech act into their notebooks, e.g., *"I will have to order food at a restaurant (Requesting)."* Students will take these notebooks with them overseas and write reflections about the situations they encounter. They should note how successful they felt their interaction was, any language difficulties or misunderstandings they had, and how they might perform better next time. If students can identify the phrases, vocabulary, or grammar that they are having difficulty with, they can then consult with somebody in the target community for help. These habits of self-monitoring, reflection, and action should assist learners on their journey to becoming more autonomous learners.

Conclusion

The Japanese government has stated its aim to double the number of students studying abroad by 2020 in order to "meet the demand for talented individuals who can take part in the ever globalizing world" (MOFA, 2015). Yet our research, and that of others (e.g., Gebhard, 2013; Wang, 2009), tells us that simply sending students abroad and hoping for the best is far from enough. In order for our students to succeed while abroad and remain motivated learners of English upon their return, pre- and post-SA training sessions need to be carefully developed.

We know that the linguistic gains made on SA can quickly be lost if students lose motivation when they return and choose not to continue their studies. In large programs, it is easy for students like these to be left behind. The voices of our students instruct us to view study abroad as a "long game" that requires goal setting and visualization prior to departure, and follow-up reinforcement upon return. That is, rather than taking a universal approach where one-size-fits-all, each student's story should be listened to and taken into account in order to create more tailored instruction.

Students want to have successful interactions while overseas, and teachers naturally want to prepare them to do so. Teachers, however, may be left wondering if they have done enough to provide learners with the linguistic, social, and intercultural tools needed to succeed. We have argued in this chapter that pragmatic skills are not given enough attention in study-abroad preparation courses. We believe that the incorporation of speech acts can help to raise students' awareness of the societal norms of the cultures in which they will find themselves.

Furthermore, learners need to know that their views are valuable in shaping programs of study-abroad support, a position that encompasses a needs analysis perspective and encourages targeted instruction. Our point is that the value of study abroad should be acknowledged more. It can lay a foundation for future friendships, intercultural understandings, and, we hope, a lifetime of appreciation not only for language but also for lasting curiosity about all that the world has to offer.

Mark Firth is an assistant professor at J. F. Oberlin University in Tokyo.

James Broadbridge is an assistant professor at J. F. Oberlin University in Tokyo.

Joseph Siegel, PhD, is an associate professor at Meiji Gakuin University in Tokyo.

ACKNOWLEDGEMENT

This work was supported by JSPS KAKENHI Grant Number 26770200.

References

Fryer, M. (2012). Motivating learners for study abroad: Strategies for facilitating L2 motivation and acquisition. *Ryugaku: Explorations in Study Abroad, 5*(2), 2–14.

Gebhard, J. G. (2013). EFL learners studying abroad: Challenges and strategies. *The Asian EFL Journal Quarterly, 15*(3), 155–182.

Ishihara, N., & Cohen, A. D. (2010). *Teaching and learning pragmatics: Where language and culture meet.* Boston, MA: Pearson Education.

Kinginger, C., & Farrell, K. (2004). Assessing development of meta-pragmatic awareness in study abroad. *Frontiers: The Interdisciplinary Journal of Study Abroad, 10*, 19–42.

Ministry of Foreign Affairs of Japan. Student Exchange Program. (2015) Retrieved from http://www.mofa.go.jp/policy/culture/people/student/

Siegel, J. (2015). Using speech acts to inform study abroad instruction. *The Language Teacher, 39*(6), 3–9.

Siegel, J., & Broadbridge, J. (2016). Message sent, message received? Teachers and target community members decide. *Innovation in Language Learning and Teaching, 10*(1), 116. doi: 10.1080/17501229.2016.1143475

Taguchi, N. (2015). Instructed pragmatics at a glance: Where instructional studies, were, are, and should be going. *Language Teaching, 48*(1), 1–50.

Wang, J. (2009). A study of resiliency characteristics in the adjustment of international graduate students at American universities. *Journal of Studies in International Education, 13*(1), 22–45.

Appendix

Situation cards for developing speech-act performance

SPEECH ACT	LESS FORMAL	MORE FORMAL
Apologizing	You and your friend, Jessica, are working on a class project together. You meet Jessica at school cafeteria to talk about the project. You forgot to bring notes from class that you promised to bring to the meeting. What do you say?	You were supposed to have a meeting with your professor, Ms. Jones, at 1.00 pm today. The time is now 1.30 and you have arrived late for the meeting. What do you say to Professor Jones?
Complimenting	You are taking an American literature class. A good friend of yours, Kathy, has just made an excellent presentation in class today. After class, you want to compliment her on her performance. What do you say to Kathy?	You are staying with your homestay family. Their neighbor, Mr. Jackson, is an elderly man, who you occasionally say hello to. You see him today and he is dressed in a very smart suit as if he is going to a party. What do you say to Mr. Jackson?
Thanking	You and your close friend, Molly, are taking the same Spanish class. You misplaced your textbook so you borrowed Molly's textbook over the weekend to do your homework. You return the book to Molly on Monday. What do you say to her?	It is the end of the last class of the semester in your English writing class. You have enjoyed the course a great deal and feel that your writing skills have improved a large amount. As you are leaving the room you stop to talk to your teacher, Ms. Smith to tell her how you feel about the class. What do you say?

SECTION 3:
VOICES ON APPROACH AND COLLABORATION IN CLASSROOMS

11 Exploring Multiple Feedback Loops in EFL Writing Classes

GORDON BLAINE WEST, IN COLLABORATION WITH LEARNERS SUN A KIM, JUYOUNG SONG, AND CHAE-EUN (CATHY) SUNG

Students in English as a Foreign Language writing classes often have questions about tasks their teachers set for them: "Why do we need to edit our own work?," "Isn't that just a waste of time?," "We never know what to say when we give peer feedback because we aren't experts. Isn't it just better for the instructor to tell us what we need to change?"

In this chapter, we (the four coauthors—an instructor and three first-year university students) address such concerns by describing our process of doing peer- and self-editing in an academic EFL writing class. First, we will describe the rationale for doing peer- and self-editing in academic writing. We will then share some specific concerns students had about the editing process before detailing how the process was revised to address those concerns. Finally, we'll reflect on what we learned from the experience, as well as make some recommendations for other instructors considering peer- and self-editing in writing classes.

Rationale for Peer- and Self-Editing

Peer- and self-editing have long been integral parts of English as a Second/Foreign Language writing classes. Both processes have been shown to be beneficial to students, yet problematic to successfully implement. While peer-editing has been critiqued for providing only surface-level feedback and for giving comments that do not aid in revision (Leki, 1990), it is also true that when students are trained in giving peer feedback, it can have positive effects (Berg, 1999). For instance, peer revision can lead not only to improved writing on the part of the author receiving feedback but also to improvements in the reviewer's own writing (Lundstrom & Baker, 2009).

While self-editing might not have as big of an impact on error reduction (Diab, 2010; Ferris & Roberts, 2001), it is still an important component of an L2 writing class in helping students reflect on their writing (Ferris & Hedgcock, 2013). Despite these positive effects, teachers and researchers have noted several concerns in implementing successful peer- and self-editing components in their academic writing classes, including time constraints and other practical matters, student characteristics and cultural challenges, affective factors, and uncertainty over teachers' roles in the process (Ferris & Hedgcock, 2013; Rollinson, 2005).

Both peer- and self-editing are useful in writing classes that focus on process writing. Rather than having the focus on the final product, process writing draws attention to how writing is done and how it can be improved through revision. Editing and multiple revisions encourage students to focus not only on language development but also on the development of their writing skills. In short, peer- and self-editing play an important role, along with targeted feedback from instructors, in helping students improve their writing.

Student Concerns With the Process

As students, we had some worries about peer- and self-editing at first. The first time, our class did the editing exercises with a narrative essay. At that time, we had never received such detailed feedback, so we were a little nervous. When we were in middle and high school, many teachers tried peer- or self-editing, but it did not work very well because the students' attitudes were negative to the process.

In Korea, evaluation is almost completely limited to teachers. Having experienced this type of class for almost 10 years, our writing classmates felt generally apathetic toward the process at first and the atmosphere of our class was heavy. Even speaking our own opinions in front of our classmates was hard for us.

In our view, it is challenging work to share our writing and get feedback from students who take the same class. One of our main concerns, besides sharing our opinions generally, was wondering if we have enough skills or ability to evaluate others. We had to assume that everyone worked hard to write their papers. When we reviewed papers honestly, we could accidentally hurt their feelings by harshly evaluating their writing without even fully understanding how we were giving feedback.

At first, we could not understand why we should do self-editing. We thought it was kind of a waste of time. Why should we have to read our writing again? We did our best to write it the first time, so we thought it would be impossible to find fault in our own writing since our ability was not high enough to catch errors.

Peer- and Self-Editing Process

This section describes the peer- and self-editing processes carried out in lessons. Many of the student concerns detailed above are echoed in different contexts as well (i.e., Tsui & Ng, 2000; Zhang, 1995). Going into the class, I (the instructor) understood the concerns that my students would have and actively worked with them to design a process that would help peer- and self-editing to be successful and productive for them.

Before discussing the details of how we would do the peer-editing, I gave the class a sample essay, which we peer-edited together, following advice from researchers that training is needed before peer-editing can be successful (Min, 2005). Students were required to give two types of feedback: general comments written on the paper, and answers to specific questions on a worksheet.

On a handout I distributed to the students (Appendix A), there were sentence frames to help them write comments in a constructive way: for example, "I like how you describe . . . ," or "I am not sure what you mean by . . . , can you say this in a different way?" On the worksheet, specific questions about the paper also referred to lessons we had in class, such as, "What is the hook?," "What do you like about the beginning of the paper?," and "Is there anything you would change about the hook?" Students spent an entire class working alone, then in pairs, and finally as a large group learning how to peer-edit.

Next, we discussed how students would feel most comfortable doing peer-editing. Most agreed that some degree of anonymity would make them the most comfortable. I did not want complete anonymity however, because I explained if the person receiving the comments could not understand them, it would be necessary to ask for clarification.

Finally, we agreed that students would bring two copies of their paper to class on the due date. The copies would not have their names on them. To help students feel confident giving feedback, I made them work in pairs. They jointly gave feedback about one paper at a time. I collected and randomly distributed the student essays to each peer-editing pair, and that way each pair coedited two papers during the class. Everyone could confer with a partner before giving feedback, and everyone would get feedback from two reviewers.

For the self-editing, students were given a worksheet with 10 specific questions to answer. These included questions like, "How many sentences are in each paragraph?" and "How many transition words did you use?" These were designed to encourage students to look closely at their own writing. Other prompts encouraged them to critically consider the peer comments by asking them which comments they agreed with and which they were unsure of, as well as which things the peer reviewers agreed with or commented on. This process was designed to help writers make decisions about what revisions to make.

At the end of the process, they turned in all of the materials (peer- and self-editing sheets, a first draft, and a second draft of the essay) for me to check. Only at this stage did I give my feedback. After receiving my feedback, they did one last revision before submitting a final draft. We completed this process for both a narrative essay and an argumentative essay.

Student Reflections on Peer- and Self-Editing

One of the best things we gained through the editing process was the chance to hear peers' various opinions about our papers. We got to learn that there are many other perspectives on the same essay. It was fun to know how others thought about our expressions, and it was a great chance to widen our own viewpoints. It was also helpful to find some mistakes that we couldn't find on our own easily.

Furthermore, it was good to have a chance to learn how to listen and accept readers' opinions. Sometimes, when we got peers' feedback, the way we planned to develop our writing and the way that peers suggested were different. To solve this problem, we tried to think of a compromise. We realized that evaluating classmates who have a similar level of English helped us to develop our writing skills. We could understand why our classmates had written an incorrect expression, or used incorrect grammar or vocabulary, better than the instructor sometimes because we had made the same mistakes before. This increased our confidence as writers.

The feedback worksheets for both peer- (Appendix A) and self-editing (Appendix B) helped us think deeply about the writing and give more specific feedback to our peers. For example, with the narrative essay, the questions given on the self-analysis worksheet focused on the peer comments we received, like "What changes do you want to make after reading the comments from peers?" Questions like this helped us reconsider the comments we got. Moreover, the peer feedback sheets were filled with language prompts.

We did not know how to self-edit our own writing the first time. However, the worksheet helped us know what to focus on and how to look at the organization of the essay. The focus was different for each paper. For the narrative essay, the most helpful part of self-editing was looking at all of our verbs and the tense we used. After doing self-editing seriously, we realized that making errors with verb tense can make it difficult to understand sometimes.

Some of the problems we experienced with peer-editing were that it was difficult to do the peer-editing between classmates who were at different levels. Even though we can all learn from each other, sometimes the effectiveness of the editing could be lowered by those who did not take the activity seriously. Also, it was difficult not to feel like we were hurting feelings still when giving feedback. With some practice evaluating other essays, our skills seemed to improve.

Another problem for some of us was that when evaluating with a partner, the process was less meaningful, since the feedback from two people was almost the exact same. In some cases, when working with a partner, we tended to take the lead of the more dominant person and just write the same comments without fully evaluating the paper ourselves. This helped us avoid feeling burdened, but also limited what we learned from the activity.

Teacher Reflections on Peer- and Self-Editing

There were three main things that I, as an instructor, took away from this experience. First, although I thought I was communicating well with my students, anticipating their needs and listening to their concerns, there were still problems I did not see until the semester ended. Second, the needs and wants of the students were at times contradictory, and I had to figure out how to balance them. Third, although much of the recent research on peer- and self-editing highlights positive impacts, many older studies that raised concerns about the processes remain valid (Carson & Nelson, 1996; Leki, 1990).

At the beginning, I anticipated that some students would doubt their ability to provide useful feedback and be wary of hurting each other's feelings or losing face. Even with all of the negotiation about the process that we did in the class, I realize now that there were other ways I could have sought feedback after the initial discussion. Surveys and written feedback from questionnaires were the main ways in which I received input from students, but those methods, especially because they were written in English, were not always the best ways to get their input.

In hindsight, I should have tried other methods, such as an appointed class representative who could have acted as a sort of liaison. Students can be more comfortable approaching a fellow student, who can then pass along concerns to the instructor. Another method could have been to have students discuss the process in small groups, sharing their opinions after they felt confident that they were supported by their group.

Another issue was figuring out how best to deal with differing wants and needs of students. Many times in a compulsory general English class, the students have widely differing majors, interests, and needs. It was difficult for me to find a good balance between students who wanted the peer feedback process to be completely anonymous versus those who would rather have it face-to-face, or those who wanted more self-editing versus those who wanted none. I'm still not sure how to achieve that balance. Doing it again, I would be careful to seek the opinions of those students who were quiet and not assume that deciding such issues by majority rule is the best approach.

Finally, it was hard for me to gauge exactly how successful the peer- and self-editing was in terms of advancing my students' writing skills. I believe the more recent research that says peer-editing helps students improve their writing (Diab, 2010; Ludstrom & Baker, 2009), or that self-editing is important in helping students reflect more on their writing (Ferris & Hedgcock, 2013).

However, it also seems clear that older research that highlighted some major concerns with peer- and self-editing remains valid. Examples of this are students not trusting each other's comments or their own ability to give feedback (Carson & Nelson, 1996), which was an on-going concern that was never completely resolved in my class. Furthermore, some of Leki's (1990) comments about peer-feedback being superficial applied to our class, as evidenced by some students only commenting "good" or "nice work" about their peer's papers. The newer research can help us understand why we should do peer- and self-editing in classes, but the older concerns should also help inform how we as instructors go about implementing the process.

Students' Suggestions

After doing peer- and self-editing, we would like to make some suggestions from a student perspective. First, as we mentioned before, it is best to practice the editing process regularly. By this, we mean to have more practice before and during editing, as well as doing more editing in class. This can help students feel more natural giving their own opinion on others' essays.

Not having anonymity was something that many of us were uncomfortable with. One option is having students do the peer-editing at home, where it can be totally anonymous. Another benefit of doing the editing at home is that we have more time to read and give careful feedback.

Some felt that doing the editing at home would also be good, but did not want to increase anonymity. Rather, we could have class time for oral feedback conferences about the papers. For example, after getting back our writing with others' comments on it, we can first read through all of the comments. Then we can ask questions and get answers from each commenter. Through that process, the feeling that we might have hurt each other written in comments would be reduced because we can sit face-to-face and make our opinions and thoughts clearer.

Perhaps the peer-editing should be graded. Some students just wrote "great" or "good." But such simple feedback isn't helpful. By having the activity graded, the instructor can better control the quality of peer-editing that happens in the class.

Teachers' Suggestions

Each instructor at our university has a different approach to doing peer- and self-editing. Some have students do all editing at home. Others take much more class time to do the editing. Still others have conferences with students after the editing process to discuss changes one-on-one. The thing that all instructors agreed on, however, is that the process needs to be constantly evaluated and adjusted.

Getting students involved in the decision-making and design process is vital. Teachers should also search for different ways to get feedback and understand the process from the students' perspectives throughout the course, not simply at the beginning or the end. This helps to get buy-in from the students on the process, because students need to see a clear benefit to the work and feel comfortable enough to trust the process and genuinely engage in the editing work.

Gordon Blaine West is an assistant professor of Young Learner–TESOL at Sookmyung Women's University.

Sun A Kim studies Korean language & literature at Sookmyung Women's University.

Juyoung Song studies Chinese literature and language at Sookmyung Women's University.

Chae Eun (Cathy) Sung studies business administration at Ewha Women's University.

References

Berg, E. C. (1999). The effects of trained peer response on ESL students' revision types and writing quality. *Journal of Second Language Writing, 8*(3), 215–241.

Carson, J. G., & Nelson, G. L. (1996). Chinese students' perceptions of ESL peer response group interaction. *Journal of Second Language Writing, 5*(1), 1–19.

Diab, N. M. (2010). Effects of peer-versus self-editing on students' revision of language errors in revised drafts. *System, 38*(1), 85–95.

Ferris, D. R., & Hedgcock, J. (2013). *Teaching L2 composition: Purpose, process, and practice*. New York, NY: Routledge.

Ferris, D., & Roberts, B. (2001). Error feedback in L2 writing classes: How explicit does it need to be? *Journal of Second Language Writing, 10*(3), 161–184.

Leki, I. (1990). Potential problems with peer responding in ESL writing classes. *CATESOL Journal, 3*(1), 5–19.

Lundstrom, K., & Baker, W. (2009). To give is better than to receive: The benefits of peer review to the reviewer's own writing. *Journal of Second Language Writing, 18*(1), 30–43.

Min, H. T. (2005). Training students to become successful peer reviewers. *System, 33*(2), 293–308.

Rollinson, P. (2005). Using peer feedback in the ESL writing class. *ELT Journal, 59*(1), 23–30.

Tsui, A. B., & Ng, M. (2000). Do secondary L2 writers benefit from peer comments? *Journal of Second Language Writing, 9*(2), 147–170.

Zhang, S. (1995). Reexamining the affective advantage of peer feedback in the ESL writing class. *Journal of Second Language Writing, 4*(3), 209–222.

Appendix A: Argumentative Essay Peer-Editing Worksheet Questions

Argument Essay Peer Feedback

1) First, read the whole paper.

2) Think about the paper—what are your feelings after reading it?

3) Go through each sentence and each paragraph again and write comments or questions directly on the paper.

> Some examples:
>
> > I really like this sentence because......
> >
> > I think this word/phrase is useful because.......
> >
> > I liked how you described.......
> >
> > > or
> >
> > What do you mean by "-------"?
> >
> > I don't understand this word/phrase. Could you please explain?
> >
> > I'm not sure what you mean by this. Could you make it clearer?
> >
> > I think you can add more details here.
> >
> > I think you can write more about ". . ." here.

* *

After writing comments on the paper, answer the following questions.

1) What is the author's thesis?

2) What is the hook? What kind of hook is it? Can the hook be more interesting? How?

3) What are the main arguments in the paper?

4) How many sentences are in each paragraph? Is the paper well-developed with lots of evidence and supporting details? Where does it need more?

5) What transitions does the author use? Can you think of any different transitions? Write your suggestions on the paper.

6) Are there any opposing viewpoints in the essay? If yes, write them here. If not, write a counter argument to the author's thesis.

7) What suggestions do you have for the writer about this essay? What parts need more support or are unclear?

Appendix B: Argumentative Essay Self-Editing Worksheet Questions

Argument Essay Self Review

1. What is your thesis?

2. Do you support your thesis? How so? List your arguments.

3. How many sentences are in each body paragraph? Is there a topic sentence telling your arguments? Are there a few sentences of supporting evidence or examples? List how many sentences are in each paragraph (i.e., para. 1 = 8 sentences, para. 2 = 4 sentences, etc.)

4. Is each example or supporting detail explained? For example, after you tell an example, is there a sentence telling why that example is important or necessary for the reader to know? Give an example of one of your explanations of supporting details.

5. What transitions do you use? List them here.

6. Do you give any opposing viewpoints in your paper? Do you make counter-arguments against them? Give examples.

7. Read the paper again—look especially at your verbs. Are they all the correct tense? List any you are unsure of here.

8. Read the paper one more time. This time check for vocabulary. Are there any words you need the dictionary to help you add? Are you sure you used them correctly? Write any words you are unsure of here.

9. Is your paper unified (about one big argument), coherent (following in correct order of arguments with supporting details), and developed (enough evidence)? Which one of these are you unsure about and why?

10. Reading your paper again, what part do you want to change? Why?

"I learn listening skill to get high marks": Student Voices About Listening Instruction in Vietnam

NGA THI HANG NGO AND HOA THI MAI NGUYEN

A cross the world, the English language has become increasingly more important due to globalization. As a result, many countries in Asia, including Vietnam, have implemented English-language education reforms. In Vietnam, the National Foreign Language Project 2020 aims to boost the English proficiency of Vietnamese youth to advance industrialization and modernization for the country. However, English proficiency of university graduates is still a major concern (e.g., Mai & Iwashita, 2012). Tran (2013) observes, "when leaving universities, many graduates could not communicate in English in some simple situations, they could not understand general news in English either" (p. 143). She (2013) believes that this situation is the result of the traditional examination system and teaching methods that are teacher centered and focus on reading comprehension and grammar. Current teaching practice appears to prevent students from developing other communicative skills such as listening (S. T. Le, 2011).

Among the four skills in second- and foreign-language (ESL, EFL) learning for communicative purposes, listening is considered the most vital. The teaching of listening, however, has been problematic (e.g., Field, 2012; Vandergrift, 2011). One of the concerns is with methodology. For example, Graham, Santos, and Vanderplank (2011) found in their study that teachers who regard listening as a skill to practice, not develop, simply asked students to complete listening tasks as explained in textbooks. There has been a lack of empirical research looking specifically at what teachers do in their listening lessons and how students perceive the listening instruction they receive.

This motivated us to explore the listening instruction currently provided in Vietnam. We wanted to explore students' perceptions towards classroom practice and teachers' teaching practices. This chapter reports part of a larger research project, which was to explore Vietnamese students' experiences in their EFL listening lessons over a number of years.

The Study

Using a case study research design, we carried out this study at a higher education institute in Vietnam to explore students' perceptions toward EFL learning in their listening classes. Twenty-three second-year EFL students, who ranged in age from 19 to 21, volunteered to participate in the study. They learned English in grades 6 to 11, typical for Vietnamese students prior to entering university. Their listening proficiency was at the B1 level according to the Common European Framework of Reference for Languages (CEFR) (Council of Europe, 2001), and they were required to achieve C1 level, the national goal, by the time they graduated. Listening skills were taught separately from other language skills, with two classes (100 minutes each) a week for seven semesters. They were enrolled in their second semester of listening courses while participating in our study.

These students came from different provinces in the remote areas of northwest Vietnam. This diversity allowed us to gather rich and detailed perceptions of learning from a small number of participants. All names mentioned in our study are pseudonyms. We collected data from focus groups of four to five students each.

We opted to conduct focus group interviews with open-ended questions in Vietnamese to avoid language barriers. Our aim was to explore the participants' experiences in EFL listening classes. All the interviews were transcribed and theme coded inductively using Nvivo version 10.

Findings

Two major themes emerged from the focus group discussions.

Student Voices on Teaching Procedures

Although the students came from different areas of Vietnam before they entered the university, all of them shared a similar experience in listening lessons, which consisted of listening to audio tapes. They described their teacher's main activity as playing the tapes and checking their answers. The following responses were typical:

❝ Teacher played the tape for us to listen and checked the answers. ❞ (Lai)

❝ Teacher asked us to read the instruction, listen. After that, she checked the answers when we finished listening. ❞ (Minh)

It seems that the goal of listening in class was to give the right answers. Nhi shared: "Teacher checked each student's answers and asked us to write the answers on the board." This process did not seem to facilitate interaction among learners and teachers and particularly failed to enhance a deep understanding of what the students had heard. Another student echoed Nhi's sentiments:

❝ When we listened in class, teacher asked us to open the textbook and read the questions. After checking that we understood the questions, teacher played the tapes. What we did was to listen and complete the tasks. When we finished, teacher gave answers, she did not give us chance to check or discuss the answers with each other. ❞ (Nhai)

The procedure of "listen and check" is similar to the process of testing listening. As a result, students complained that they had few chances to justify and evaluate their answers. For example, Vui further explained, "teacher only gave the answers so we did not know why we got the right or wrong answers." Thom also commented, "teacher let us listen two or three times and checked the answers. She did not care whether we understood or not." Expressing a similar opinion, Hoang recalled, "teacher sat in the stage, we sat and listened. Teacher asked us whether we completed the tasks. She never pointed out the mistakes that we made."

The goal of these types of classroom listening activities is to put students under pressure and train them to do well on listening examinations rather than enhance their skill of communicative understanding. The following comments lend support to this claim:

❝ I learn listening skill to complete the tasks. ❞ (Nam)

❝ When I could not complete the listening tasks, I copied the answers in the answer keys part because I was afraid of being asked to give the answers by the teacher. I think other students did the same. I felt very stressful of the results. ❞ (Nhai)

❝ I learn listening skill to get high marks. ❞ (Nam)

Teacher Voices on Teaching Practice

Since we are both listening teachers and teacher-trainers in Vietnam, we have had opportunities to observe English-listening classes at both high schools and universities. What the students experienced was similar to our own experiences.

One of the reasons for the prevalence of this style of lesson is the mismatch between curriculum and time allocation. The teachers need to cover all the content in the textbook in a limited class time. Another reason is that the class size of 40 to 45 students makes working in pairs and small groups more challenging.

Furthermore, in the standard classroom, the teachers control the cassette players. When we, the authors, have taught listening classes with many students but just one cassette player as the only teaching equipment, we were inclined to conduct whole class activities. This pattern is reflected in a study by Nguyen (2009) in Vietnam, which revealed that individual schools and teachers decide what students learn in the classroom. Moreover, a possible explanation for this is that teachers may lack strategies to differentiate the students' listening proficiency and needs, which results in a single one-size-fits-all approach.

Not equipping teachers with different approaches to teaching listening might also limit teachers to the product-teaching approach. As insiders, we know that teachers in this rural area are not provided with sufficient training. Therefore, they may not know how to engage students in their listening classes.

This observation coincides with findings from Bui and Nguyen's (2016) study, which found that teachers lacked confidence in teaching listening. As university educators, we believe that one of the desirable goals of teaching listening is to facilitate students' ability to listen critically and prepare them for the real-life listening activities. However, this has not been emphasized in professional development programs for Vietnamese teachers.

Students were critical of the product-teaching approach. This is understandable when the students have to frequently repeat the same procedures in every listening lesson. The following comments illustrate this point:

❝ I felt bored like in the hell. ❞ (Lai)

❝ I felt sleepy. ❞ (Hang)

❝ Listen and check, check, and check are so boring. ❞ (Thom)

These comments reveal the shortcomings of an exclusively listening product approach. They provide ample evidence supporting Field (2012) and Vandergrift (2011) that listening for the purpose of getting the right answers leads to high anxiety and low motivation. This passive listening approach tests listening ability rather than learning how to listen (Field, 2012). Despite this, the product approach is widely used in teaching listening in Vietnam and other Asian countries (Chen, 2009; Siegel, 2014).

Student and Teacher Voices on Listening Materials

Limited access to listening resources was among the common complaints by the participant students. The textbook was said to be the only material the students used in lessons. The following are typical complaints from the students about listening materials:

❝ Listening materials were limited, we only listened to one or two listening textbooks. **❞** (Huong)

❝ We had no references, only a textbook. **❞** (Ngan)

Hang, a hardworking student, further elaborated that if she listened to the text beforehand, she could not learn anything new in class because her teachers merely followed the textbook. This tells us that the traditional method did not offer students abundant exposure to other listening texts. This is similar to findings by Chen (2009) and Siegel (2014) that a teacher-centered approach limits the opportunities students have to listen to a variety of texts.

As university lecturers, we realise that although teachers at Vietnam's tertiary institutions are allowed to adapt the textbook, their view is "the textbook is law" (V. C. Le, 2011, p. 223). Overdependence on textbooks can be due to insufficient facilities. The first author (Ngo) had experience in using the Internet as a material resource when teaching listening for this group of EFL students. The biggest challenge was the lack of facilities for using videos or other material resources. To prepare for a 90-minute listening lesson with extracurricular materials, she needed a whole week as she struggled to download materials, make copies, and borrow a projector. And even with such thorough preparation, she sometimes had to cancel her lesson because of some technical issue; for example, the electricity was off or the sound was not good. Moreover, in many remote areas of Vietnam, the Internet is not available at schools. No electricity is available in some areas.

In addition, the textbook topics are often irrelevant to the students' interests and background knowledge.

❝ The topics in the textbooks were boring. **❞** (Huong)

❝ Sometimes I had to listen to very unfamiliar topics that I found hard to understand. **❞** (Ngan)

Bui (2013) also found that rural Vietnamese students were not motivated to learn English because the topics and materials were not relevant to their daily lives. This can be explained by the use of commercial textbooks such as *Impact Listening* and *Extra-listening*. Books like these cover topics for EFL students in general, not for those in a specific context. As EFL teachers in Vietnam, we know that materials need contextualization or localization to make them meaningful to students.

Implications for Teaching Listening

The findings above show that listening skill instruction in this context needs improvement. We therefore suggest some principles for improving the teaching of listening skills.

- Learners' needs should be investigated, including their favourite listening genres and topics, their listening proficiency levels, and their listening difficulties. This important step is omitted in most listening courses in Vietnam because teachers usually start with fixed curriculum provided by the institution.

- Materials adaptation is associated with the investigation of learner needs. For example, if the listening texts are challenging, the teachers need to modify the listening tasks to match the students' levels of listening proficiency with the task. Since the contents of listening topics in textbooks might be unfamiliar, teachers will need to design pre-listening activities that can link the topics to the students' experiences.

- With the introduction of modern technology, teachers can exploit a wide range of listening materials, from audio recordings to video (Field, 2012; Vandergrift, 2011). Moreover, teachers can find a huge number of listening materials on the Internet. Teachers can also have students provide listening materials by requiring them to bring their favourite English songs or movies to share with their classmates.

- Time for interaction among students and between students and teachers needs to be allotted in lessons. That is, apart from individual listening, students need to share with and get support from their peers and teachers to fully comprehend the listening texts.

- Listening practice should be extended beyond the classroom (see Nunan & Richards, 2015). More authentic listening tasks, which require the students to listen outside their classroom, should be encouraged to develop listening ability and motivation for their real-life listening. Listening strategy training is recommended to provide students with more independent listening skills and autonomy in developing their listening comprehension.

Implications for Teacher Training and Development

We believe that teachers in Vietnam need to learn much more about the theory of teaching listening, as well as build up their capacity to implement flexible approaches in their classes. In short, they need situated teacher development workshops.

The voices of the student participants in this chapter reflect a distinct need for changes in teaching methodology. As teacher-educators in Vietnam, we have recently had opportunities to redesign EFL methodology courses, including teaching listening skills to novice EFL teachers and workshops for teachers to upgrade their teaching skills. In order to contextualize the theories of teaching, we designed a listening skills module, which focuses on three major elements: awareness raising, implementation practice, and reflection.

Awareness raising stresses the importance of increasing teachers' awareness of listening instruction by providing student teachers with the theoretical knowledge of different teaching strategies and how to employ them. Implementation practice refers to the actual application of the teaching techniques through microteaching or during their practicum. The third major element, reflection, is a means of constantly examining their thoughts about connections between theory and practice.

Teachers have told us that what they gained from the workshops was very practical because they had opportunities to implement theory and later to reflect on these teaching approaches. Teacher participants shared that without practicing the approaches introduced in professional development programs and evaluating their own teaching practice, it is not possible to gain deeper understanding of how theories might work in practice. It seems to us that the missing link in teacher education programs in most contexts is the authentic voices of teachers and students. This calls for developing teachers' agency for change in their context by providing them with life-long learning skills, including the ability to reflect on how practice can inform theory.

....

Nga Thi Hang Ngo is a doctoral candidate at the University of Sydney, Australia, and a lecturer in TESOL at Tay Bac University, Vietnam.

Hoa Thi Mai Nguyen is a lecturer in Teacher Professional Learning and TESOL at the School of Education, University of New South Wales, Australia.

References

Bui, T. N. T. (2013). *"Can a basket hide an elephant?"—Language policy and practices toward linguistic, educational, and socio-economic equity in Vietnam.* (Unpublished doctoral dissertation.) University of Hawaii at Manoa, United States.

Bui, T. N. T., & Nguyen, H. T. M. (2016). Standardizing English for educational and socio-economic betterment: A critical analysis of English language policy reforms in Vietnam. In R. Kirkpatrick (Ed.), *English language education policy in Asia* (pp. 363–388). Switzerland: Springer International Publishing.

Chen, A. (2009). Listening strategy instruction: Exploring Taiwanese college students' strategy development. *Asian EFL Journal, 11*(2), 54–85.

Council of Europe. (2001). *Common European framework of reference for languages: Learning, teaching and assessment.* Cambridge, England: Cambridge University Press.

Field, J. (2012). Listening instruction. In A. R. Burns (Ed.), *Pedagogy and practice in second language teaching* (pp. 207–217). New York, NY: Cambridge University Press.

Graham, S., Santos, D., & Vanderplank, R. (2011). Exploring the relationship between listening development and strategy use. *Language Teaching Research, 15*(4), 435–456. doi: 10.1177/1362168811412026

Le, S. T. (2011). *Teaching English in Vietnam: Improving the provision in the private sector.* (Unpublished doctoral thesis.) Victoria University, New Zealand.

Le, V. C. (2011). *Form-focused instruction: A case study of Vietnamese teachers' beliefs and practices.* (Unpublished doctoral thesis.) University of Waikato, New Zealand.

Mai, N. K., & Iwashita, N. (2012). A comparison of learners' and teachers' attitudes toward communicative language teaching at two universities in Vietnam. *University of Sydney Papers in TESOL, 7,* 25–49.

Nguyen, H. T. M. (2009). An experimental application of the problem-posing approach for English language teaching in Vietnam. In T. Stewart (Ed.), *Insights on teaching speaking in TESOL* (pp. 79–90). Alexandria, VA: TESOL, Inc.

Nunan, D., & Richards, J. C. (Eds.). (2015). *Language learning beyond the classroom.* New York, NY: Routledge.

Siegel, J. (2014). Exploring L2 listening instruction: Examinations of practice. *ELT Journal, 68*(61), 22–30. doi:10.1093/elt/cct058

Tran, T. T. (2013). Factors affecting teaching and learning English in Vietnamese university. *The Internet Journal of Language, Culture and Society, 38,* 138–145.

Vandergrift, L. (2011). Second language listening: Presage, process, product, and pedagogy. In E. Hinkel (Ed.), *Handbook of research in second language teaching and learning* (pp. 455–472). New York, NY: Routledge.

13 Dealing With Resistance to Student-Centered Instruction: The Struggles of a Japanese NNEST

RYAN W. SMITHERS AND RIE SMITHERS

> **❝** Student-centered activities like collaborative and cooperative learning don't work at lower-level universities because many of the students at these universities shouldn't be there; nor do they want to be there. They don't want to participate or do any work in or out of class, and during group work activities, they are the ones that are sleeping, playing with their smartphones, or chatting in their first language with whomever else will chat with them about anything unrelated to school or the task at hand. I hate these students. **❞**
> (Nonnative-English-speaking teacher)

If you have spent much time teaching a foreign language (FL) in tertiary classrooms, you too may know the frustrations that unmotivated and demotivated students can bring. And although you may not feel frustrated enough to say that you hate some of your students, you have likely experienced a roller coaster ride of emotions that have tested your resolve. The highs that teachers long to experience, because of how they inspire and fulfill us, could be the result of deep pedagogical knowledge, superb planning, great teaching strategies, or even excellent classroom management. More than likely, however, they are the result of sound practice guided by an ethic of caring that allows for positive connections to be made with students (Hargreaves, 1998). Conversely, unexpected opposition in the classroom to an approach or strategy can cause teachers to retreat to ineffective teaching methods in a scramble for security and stability (Felder & Brent, 1996).

Our chapter stresses the need for teachers to avoid making irrational decisions about a teaching methodology in the face of student adversity. The context is a contemporary English as a Foreign Language (EFL) classroom in higher education in Japan. The voices presented in this chapter are those of a Japanese nonnative English-speaking teacher (NNEST: second author, Rie Smithers) and her students (Japanese university EFL students). The students' voices were gathered through questionnaires and individual structured interviews. Student voices highlight the need to be sensitive to the attitudes and expectations that they bring to the learning situation, while Rie's voice speaks of a teacher's yearning to be conscientious in spite of her skepticism that a particular approach—student-centered instruction—is appropriate for her classes.

We begin with a brief description of the context in which Rie's story is framed, and then sketch the theoretical background for our narrative. After that, we analyze and theorize the various voices presented in this chapter. Finally, we conclude by echoing Holliday's (1994, p. 1) call for teachers to research their own practice so that methodology becomes "appropriate to the social context within which it is to be used."

Background

❝ I believe students have to use English to acquire English skills, so I try to provide them with time to use English in the classroom as much as possible. Also, to increase students' responsibilities and motivation, and more importantly and pragmatically, to prevent them from getting bored and falling asleep, I have them do group and pair work activities. Specifically, my students do extensive reading of texts out loud, solve comprehension questions, discuss, debate, act, or make presentations based on project work in every class. ❞ (Nonnative-English-speaking teacher)

Being a foreign-language teacher in higher education can be very challenging, and may be especially so in Japan, where students are noted for the liberties that they take. "[T]hey can play, read novels, gossip, sleep, or leave the classroom any time without receiving permission," notes Hussain (2015, p. 39). Is it possible to achieve a positive learning environment in this kind of climate? Rie believes that students who encounter student-centered learning from native-English-speaking teachers (NESTs) at universities and colleges in Japan can feel that it has life-changing potential. This was her experience as an undergraduate student. In fact, she credits the student-centered instruction she received as being the catalyst that allowed her to develop a natural motivation for lifelong learning and believes her penchant for learning and personal growth (McCombs, 1991) was awakened because a teacher provided her with a positive, student-centered learning environment that: (1) was supportive, (2) allowed for personal choice, (3) demanded that learning be her responsibility, and (4) allowed her to ascertain relevance and meaning in learning, with the end result being that she discovered the joy of learning. She shares her experience as follows:

❝ It was the first time for me to research things that I was personally interested in. I needed to read, write, ask, and think all in English to know what I wanted to know. Until then, I studied English as just one of many subjects that I had to take, so my purpose was to get a better score in English by answering fill-in-the-blank questions for some English sentences or translating on exams. English became a very convenient tool for me to gather interesting information that I was not able to find in Japanese. To know about western people, culture, or history by typing English key words on the Internet was like a new magic for me. ❞

The spell that was cast upon her was so profound that two years into her post-college career, she found herself unable to silence the voice that was calling her back to school to study for a doctorate in English literature and become a university professor. Unfortunately for her and the majority of literature majors in Japan, there are too few literature positions available, so most end up teaching a foreign language with nothing but their own formal education and language learning experiences to guide them on what constitutes sound practice (Chilton, 2016). And because teacher-centered instruction is the de facto standard for EFL education in Japan, especially at junior and senior high schools (Maehara, 2008), the majority of NNESTs today find themselves replicating this methodology that was imparted to them during their formative years.

Rie has 10 years of experience teaching EFL at *juku* (private "cram school"), high schools, and universities in Japan. She claims that the teacher-centered indoctrination begins at junior and senior high school, where students focus mainly on the grammar translation method, with speaking lessons relegated to reading words that are spelled out phonetically with *katakana*—a Japanese writing system designed to utilize Japanese phonemes. In fact, she distinctly remembers "*the blackboard written mostly in Japanese*" because "*in every class the teacher wrote down the translation of certain sentences on the blackboard, and students just copied them in their notebooks.*"

Methodological Orientation

Ideally, the purpose of a FL teaching methodology is to connect theory with how best to teach a language in a given context. Accordingly, teaching methods outline teacher roles, appropriate teaching materials, and relevant learning tasks. As a result, teaching becomes the practice of linking the features of a method to practice.

   In this section, we provide a framework (see Figure 1, below) that synthesizes the key concepts of student-centered instruction from the literature (i.e., Brown, 2003; Liu, Qiao, & Lui, 2006; Nunan, 2013) to clarify what it is that teachers like Rie are trying to accomplish when they say that they are advocates of this paradigm. As Figure 1 illustrates, student-centered teachers are not dominant in the classroom. They take on roles as coaches or facilitators and encourage students to become stakeholders in a learning process that promotes student autonomy. As such, students not only learn at their own pace but become empathetic to classroom learning objectives and are encouraged to choose what and how they learn. Learning may involve discussions, debates, brainstorming, question formulating, or explanation tasks that conclude by having students sum up and reflect on what they learned relative to their learning objectives. Finally, student-centered instruction necessitates that teachers be flexible and ask divergent or open-ended questions that open up spaces for student expression, as opposed to asking direct, rhetorical questions.

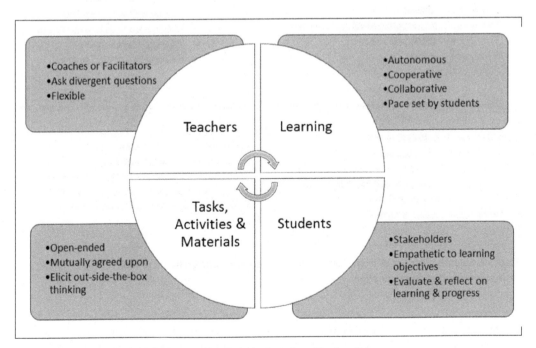

Figure 1. A framework of the key concepts of student-centered instruction.

Hostility Toward Student-Centered Instruction

The Teacher's View

In this section, we get a unique look into the struggles, and near about-face that Rie experienced. In this retelling, we hear how she has grappled with her identity as a NNEST and what it means to be a responsible teacher during a semester filled with angst over a *"lack of appreciation for the effort made to provide them* [students] *with quality lessons"* at a four-year university in Japan where she teaches compulsory EFL to false beginners in classes of 30 to 35 students.

❝ For the students at the two good universities where I teach, student-centered activities work as I intend, but for students at a lower-level university,[1] I just give them a great opportunity to goof off. These students won't join in any of the student-centered activities that I offer, and when I speak in English, they do not even try to listen. Lower-level university students in Japan don't want to be at university, let alone in my class. **❞**

It seems her assumption may be correct. Survey results (see Figure 2, below) from her classes reveal that more than two-thirds of her students attend university because they believe it is the only way to get a good job. In fact, one out of three employees in Japan today is a non-regular employee (Sugimoto, 2014). This means that prospects for stable employment are tenuous, and the students seem to know this, which may explain their resistance to classroom control.

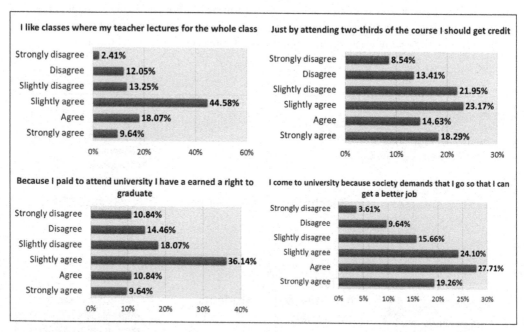

Figure 2. Selected responses from student (N = 83) survey results on items related to attitudes toward higher education.

---

[1] The lower-level university is ranked between 200–225 in the ranking of Japanese universities, while the other two universities are among the top 75, according to Webometrics Ranking of World Universities (Consejo Superior de Investigaciones Cientificas, 2015).

Kelly (1993), in his bleak appraisal of Japanese universities, recommends that teachers either teach to the few students who genuinely come to class to learn or resign themselves to the role of entertainer.

> One time, I just let the students chat and play to see how they would react to my silence. I expected them to notice right away that I was angry, but they did not, and kept talking for more than 20 minutes. Their voices eventually became so loud that I became horse [sic] shouting to get their attention. I felt terrible after this and lost my voice for a few days because of it.

Unfortunately, her attempts at integrating immediacy into her classes did not fare well, so she resorted to a control strategy that is negatively correlated with immediacy (Rocca & McCroskey, 1999)—verbal aggression.

> Afterwards, every time before student-centered activities, I felt I needed to threaten them by saying that I would give them a serious test that would be almost impossible to pass. But this also didn't work, and I often found myself yelling at them in our mother tongue to try to regain control of the class. This does not seem right, and it is very sad for me that a teacher has to threaten students to force them to study.

After failing to regain control by being stern, she made a new attempt at balancing authority with solidarity in the hope that she might somehow gain the respect of her students.

> What is more depressing is that I now accept students chatting in Japanese with their group members or partner because I have convinced myself that they are at least learning a communication skill. But there seems to be no end to these students' shame, because now during group work, some students are sleeping or playing on their smartphones.

In this next excerpt, it becomes apparent that Rie is at her wits' end and looking for closure, but is unable to find it.

> I really want to punish these rude and lazy students by giving them a terrible score or failing them, but I can't. . . . How can I fail a student based on subjective or group assessment? It seems easier for me, and fairer for all the students, if I stop doing group work and evaluate students on their performance on paper tests. This way, I will have the objective results I need to justify failing all the garbage students.

In the literature, the advantages cited of student-centered versus teacher-centered instruction far outnumber the disadvantages, and, accordingly, account for the high regard in which this approach is held in higher education today (Richards & Rogers, 2014). But is this approach truly appropriate in this context? Rie has her doubts.

> I think the individualized learning and assessment that takes place in teacher-centered classes is better suited to lower-level universities because the conscientious students that perform well in student-centered classes will also put forth enough effort to do well in teacher-centered classes.

Student Views

Holliday (1994, p. 145) stresses the importance of understanding how influences from outside the classroom might affect any conflict that occurs within. For this reason, we wanted to discover how "macro influences from outside the classroom" impacted "the micro events of classroom interaction," with an eye toward evaluating the appropriateness of student-centered instruction in this context.

To do this, we initially had Rie's students answer a 16-item questionnaire (see the Appendix) that sought to discover their attitudes toward higher education (Figure 2), learning English (Figure 3), and student-centered instruction (Figure 4). Following an analysis of this data, students were then asked to answer open-ended questions to triangulate our findings and lend their voices to the inherently impersonal nature of the survey data.

According to students at Rie's problematic, "lower-level university," the majority of them do seem to value their English education and are at least instrumentally motivated to study in her class (see Figure 3). But is their understanding of the utilitarian value and advantage of learning English motive enough to shift them toward an acceptance of student-centered instruction and increase their engagement? According to Gardner and MacIntyre (1991), integrative motivation has the most transformative power, but a perceived need for English in the future can elicit a positive effect on foreign-language learning.

When queried about their fondness for student-centered activities (Figure 4), only 17% of students expressed dislike for group work, and an even lower 14% seemed opposed to interpersonal communication with their classmates. When asked if they preferred teacher-centered lessons over student-centered ones, surprisingly, 75% of students declared approval for student-centered instruction. Ironically, a similar majority also declared their fondness for teacher-centered lectures. "*I like lectures because I hate speaking English,*" exclaims one student. "*I like lectures because they are more relaxing,*" says another.

Figure 2 is where we find the keys to unlocking the text of this classroom. According to Holliday (1994), by unlocking the text of our classroom we will find insights into the culture of our classroom. This knowledge allows teachers to question our methodology's appropriateness. In Figure 2, we see how Rie's agenda to promote a student-centered methodology could be clashing with her students' agendas. Most notable here is that apathy toward learning seems to be tied to

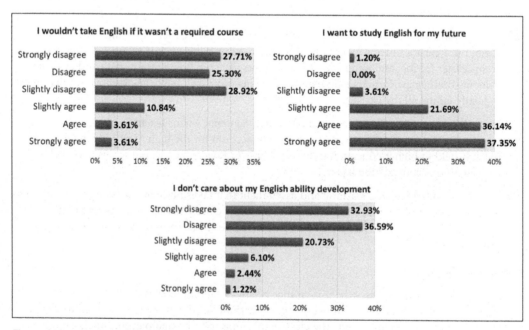

Figure 3. Selected responses from student (N = 83) survey results on items related to attitudes toward learning English.

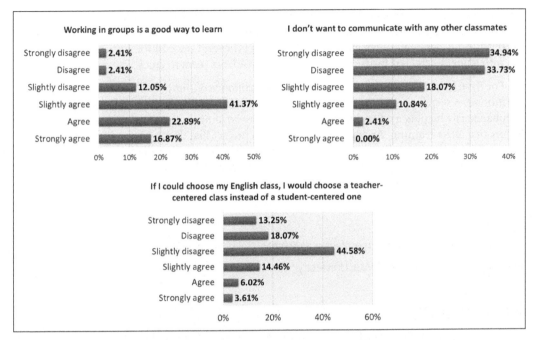

Figure 4. Selected responses from student (N = 83) survey results on items related to student-centered learning.

a sense of entitlement among these students. For some, being granted credit for simply attending two-thirds of the class is good because "*if I attend two-thirds of the classes I can understand the majority of the class contents,*" explains one student. "*Students just want to have fun so this system is good for them,*" says another. One student declares, "*I don't think it is a good idea to fail students who can't study well. We paid tuition so we should graduate.*"

Conclusion

Few things are more rewarding for classroom teachers than finding a methodology that works, i.e., fits its intended social context. Conversely, nothing is more frustrating than when problems arise from a methodology that is not appropriate for its context. Holliday (1994) argues that finding an appropriate methodology may be like trying to find a pot of gold at the end of a rainbow, but this should not preclude one from trying. In actuality, we may just discover that even though we never do find that pot of gold, the journey along the way might turn up a few prized nuggets. Likewise, trying to discover why a particular approach or method is not working does not have to be a burden. In fact, you need look no further than the pages of any TESOL-related publications to discover the benefits of researching practice.

For Rie, a newcomer to practitioner research, the quest for understanding has been fruitful. She understands that she was right to stay true to her convictions despite frustration and disillusionment from an unsavory teaching context. She also knows that there are students who genuinely want to be in her class and learn. Moreover, Rie now recognizes that most of her students are motivated to learn English and are open to some of the precepts of student-centered instruction, which will allow her to strategically move forward.

> This was a good learning experience for me—researching my practice. I learned that whatever I do, I can't satisfy all students. Poor student attitudes seem to be the result of factors from outside my classroom—Japanese society—which is beyond my control. I want to continue with student-centered instruction because most students seem to enjoy active learning.

For Ryan (first author), the senior researcher-practitioner of this collaborative practitioner-research project, mentoring a novice NNEST-researcher has been rewarding, while simultaneously helping a colleague deal with adversity by showing her how to investigate the factors that affect learning. And while a collaborative project like this can seem like a one-sided undertaking, helping a colleague work through puzzling aspects of her practice and connect the dots between theory and practice has given us both deeper understanding about the interdependent relationship that exists between theory and practice. We hope that Rie's story will resonate with many readers in this way as well.

Ryan W. Smithers is an assistant professor at Kwansei Gakuin University.

Rie Smithers is a lecturer at Kansai University.

References

Brown, K. L. (2003). From teacher-centered to learner-centered curriculum: Improving learning in diverse classrooms. *Education, 124*(1), 49–54.

Chilton, M. (2016). *English studies beyond the 'center': Teaching literature and the future of global English.* Oxon, England: Routledge.

Consejo Superior de Investigaciones Científicas. (2015). Webometrics ranking of world universities. Retrieved from http://www.webometrics.info/en/Asia/Japan

Felder, R. M., & Brent, R. (1996). Navigating the bumpy road to student-centered instruction. *College Teaching, 44,* 43–47. Retrieved from http://www.ncsu.edu/felder-public/Papers/Resist.html

Gardner, R. C., & MacIntyre, P. D. (1991). An instrumental motivation in language study: Who says it isn't effective? *Studies in Second Language Acquisition, 13*(1), 57–72. doi:10.1017/S0272263100009724

Hargreaves, A. (1998). The emotional practice of teaching. *Teaching and Teacher Education, 14*(8), 835–854. doi:10.1016/S0742-051X(98)00025-0

Holliday, A. (1994). *Appropriate methodology and social context.* Cambridge, England: Cambridge University Press.

Hussain, Z. (2015). Learning the biochemistry of English classes in Japan. *The Language Teacher, 39*(6), 38–39.

Kelly, C. (1993). The hidden role of the university. In P. Wadden (Ed.), *A handbook for teaching English at Japanese colleges and universities* (pp. 172–191). New York, NY: Oxford University Press.

Liu, R., Qiao, X., & Liu, Y. (2006). A paradigm shift of learner-centered teaching style: Reality or illusion? *Arizona Working Papers in Second Language Acquisition & Teaching, 13,* 77–91.

Maehara, Y. (2008). The effectiveness of learner-centered grammar teaching. *Journal of Foreign Language Education, 5,* 115–143.

McCombs, B. L. (1991). Motivation and lifelong learning. *Educational Psychologist, 26*(2), 117–127. doi:10.1207/s15326985ep2602_4

Nunan, D. (2013). *Learner-centered English language education: The selected works of David Nunan.* New York, NY: Routledge.

Richards, J. C., & Rodgers, T. S. (2014). *Approaches and methods in language teaching* (3rd ed.). Cambridge, England: Cambridge University Press.

Rocca, K. A., & McCroskey, J. C. (1999). The interrelationship of student ratings of instructors' immediacy, verbal aggressiveness, homophily, and interpersonal attraction. *Communication Education, 48*(4), 308–316. doi:10.1080/036345299093 79181

Sugimoto, Y. (2014). *An introduction to Japanese society* (3rd ed.). Melbourne, Australia: Cambridge University Press.

Appendix

English Learner Questionnaire

This is an anonymous questionnaire to find out what you think of the English language education you are receiving. Please answer all the questions as honestly as you can. This is not a test and your answers will not influence your grade for this class. Thank you!

Circle only **ONE** number for every question that best describes your honest feeling. <u>Please do not leave out any of the questions.</u>

Strongly agree (100% YES)	Agree (70% YES)	Slightly agree (30% YES)	Slightly disagree (30% NO)	Disagree (70% NO)	Strongly disagree (100% NO)
6	5	4	3	2	1

01. I wouldn't take English if it wasn't a required course.	6	5	4	3	2	1
02. Working by myself is better for learning than working with others in a group.	6	5	4	3	2	1
03. If I could choose my English class, I would choose a teacher-centered class instead of a student centered.	6	5	4	3	2	1
04. Having a Japanese teacher explain things in English is a waste of time.	6	5	4	3	2	1
05. I want to be able to practice speaking English in class.	6	5	4	3	2	1
06. Just by attending two-thirds of the course, I should get credit.	6	5	4	3	2	1
07. Working in groups is a good way to learn.	6	5	4	3	2	1
08. I want to study English for my future.	6	5	4	3	2	1
09. I don't care about my English ability development.	6	5	4	3	2	1
10. In the future, I will need to speak English with foreigners.	6	5	4	3	2	1
11. I like classes where my teacher lectures for the whole class.	6	5	4	3	2	1
12. I come to university because society demands that I go so that I can get a better job.	6	5	4	3	2	1
13. Because I could enter this university, I have earned the right to not have to study.	6	5	4	3	2	1
14. I don't want to communicate with any other classmates	6	5	4	3	2	1
15. Because I have paid to attend university, I have earned the right to graduate	6	5	4	3	2	1
16. Teachers that make me study are annoying.	6	5	4	3	2	1

14 Language and Content Teacher Collaboration: A Recipe for Success

AKIKO TSUDA AND DARCY DE LINT

D o you remember eating lunch at school? Does it bring back memories of healthy and tasty dishes? What did you eat? What does this have to do with language teaching, you ask? Quite simply, our chapter serves up food for thought about such matters.

Many universities worldwide have introduced English for Specific Purposes (ESP) programs to address learners' needs and improve their employability. In this chapter, we reflect on data from a longitudinal needs analysis and from our own experience of developing an ESP program for dietetic students in Japan. The key ingredient for developing this program was the collaboration among English teachers and core content area teachers, a mix that included nonnative and native-English teachers.

Generally, ESP practitioners are not familiar with the core content area. On the other hand, only a few core content teachers normally have a concrete idea of what English-language programs for their students should entail. The challenge for us was to find the most appealing recipe for collaboration amongst this diverse mix of faculty views.

Dudley-Evans and St. John (1998, pp. 5–15, 42–48) suggest three levels of cooperation when ESP specialists engage with subject-area faculty members: cooperation, collaboration, and team-teaching. Based on 10 years of experience in interdisciplinary collaboration, this chapter describes a case study of how English teachers and core content teachers developed effective teamwork through cooperation (needs analysis) and collaboration (materials development and lesson implementation).

Background

In Japan, school lunch programs are an integral part of the school experience for most public school students, and dietitians hired by local governments supervise the menus. Not all school lunch programs serve the same food, however, because the government encourages regions to include locally grown items in their fare (Fukue, 2009).

In 1952, Nakamura Gakuen Junior College was established as a dietetic training institution in Fukuoka, the fifth largest city in Japan with a population of 1.5 million. Because of its location, it is called "the gateway to Asia."

Since the college's establishment, it has served as the leading dietetics institution in western Japan. In 2006, the first author, Tsuda, a Japanese English teacher, joined the faculty as the only English as a Foreign Language teacher-coordinator. She is in charge of a course for approximately 320 dietetic students and has been collaborating with other teachers to design and implement EFL courses for them. The second author, de Lint, joined the faculty as a part-time native-English-speaking teacher in 2012.

Why Should Japanese Dietitians Learn English?

After joining the college, I (first author, Tsuda) felt isolated in monthly faculty meetings, surrounded by core content teachers. I often wondered, "Why am I teaching English to Japanese dietetic students?" Nobody had explained it to me.

In the dietetics department, the core content teachers are tenured faculty members teaching nutrition science, dietetics, biochemistry, and culinary arts. Most of them hold doctorates, and some are active in international academia. They therefore appreciate the importance of the English language to their students' prospective careers. However, when I arrived, there was no consensus among faculty members regarding English-language programs. Furthermore, due to a curriculum filled with core subjects, English-language courses were given lower priority.

The first challenge I encountered in redesigning the program was the absence of course guidelines and materials specifically designed for teaching English to dietetics students. In addition, no information from the previous English teachers was available since the course had been taught by part-time teachers and teachers from other departments. To work around this, I chose to begin by teaching English for General Purposes (EGP), which I had already taught in other programs.

A Critical Incident

My students, generally speaking, were determined to become dietitians in local communities, and were very busy studying required subjects, including lab work and cooking exercises. Core content teachers demanded that students concentrate on preparing for their one-week internships in nursery schools, hospitals, and company cafeterias, because during these internships, they needed to design nutritious lunch menus by themselves.

After a year at the college, I reflected on my lessons. Many students seemed exhausted. In addition, I overheard several miscommunications between students and a former part-time native-English-speaking teacher. One day, a student came to my office and complained, "I was interested in learning English at high school, but this college doesn't have a proper English program, does it? I'm a bit disappointed."

Apparently, our mixed-level classes of approximately 30 students were in a somewhat chaotic situation. Many times, students could not understand the native-English-speaker's instructions. In my own class, I was using a typical EFL textbook published in England that some students felt was too difficult, while others thought it too easy.

Before joining this college, I had about 10 years' experience teaching English as a part-time teacher and felt confident teaching the language. However, I had no experience collaborating with other teachers or designing a program on my own. I intentionally kept a distance from other teachers for fear of violating individual teacher's territory. But this incident with the student encouraged me to assume the role of coordinator and to redevelop the program to better meet student needs. Next, I describe that process of redeveloping the curriculum.

Teacher Collaboration

First Stage: Cooperation

Along with core content teachers, I (Tsuda) conducted a needs analysis and then worked with new native-English teachers, including de Lint (the second author), on finalizing course objectives, material selection, and classroom management.

Needs analysis. To design more practical programs, I wrote a letter to a culinary professor who served as the division chief to explain my situation. He promised to support me and suggested I conduct a needs analysis at students' future workplaces.

To collect triangulated data (see Long, 2005, pp. 28–30), I conducted an extensive needs analysis that included the following methods:

1. Unstructured interview with core content teachers.

2. Open-ended questionnaire targeting core content teachers and graduates.

3. Classroom observation.

4. Observation of core content teachers at an international conference.

5. Unstructured interviews with students' future employers and coworkers, such as nursery school principals and senior dietitians at hospitals.

6. Open-ended questionnaire targeting international students living in Fukuoka.

The data collection using the first four methods above targeted core content teachers and graduates of the college. Some of them gave me useful advice as mentors. In our institution, we have classroom observation weeks (Method 3), during which I have opportunities to observe many classes. I have also received feedback after observation by fellow teachers and administrative staff.

As a resource for needs analysis, current faculty members who graduated from the school have been particularly helpful. Most graduates had a negative impression of EFL classes when enrolled at the college. The following reply (by an associate professor in her 40s) was typical: "It was pointless. I had no idea what we were studying in a large classroom." These graduates learned English using the traditional teacher-centered Grammar Translation method. Most faculty I spoke to regarded themselves as self-taught English for Academic Purposes (EAP) learners, and some came to me for language support before attending international conventions.

The interview sessions were a good opportunity to get to know each other better and opened up unexpected pathways. In all honesty, I started the interviews for the sole purpose of needs analysis, but since many faculty members showed interest in what I was doing, I found several collaborators through these sessions. Among practical ideas for content-based instruction (CBI) in higher education, Stewart, Sagliano, and Sagliano (2002, p. 42) list identification of "faculty members who are willing to design and team teach a CBI course" as part of the first stage of teacher collaboration. Contacting interested colleagues is the initial step to successful teacher collaboration.

One professor in her 60s was quite skeptical about ESP, saying, "I'm not sure, but it might be better for colleges to teach English literature to students." I found her reaction understandable. She was taught English in a traditional way, and since then, she has been developing her academic English skills as an autonomous learner. I conducted more surveys to learn from faculty members.

Even though there was no consensus among teachers about the best methods, student needs could not be overlooked. For instance, a second-year student came to my office to ask for advice. She told me that at a job interview with a local food manufacturer, she was told to improve her

English skills before joining the company as a dietitian, most likely because the manufacturer planned to expand its international business.

Survey Methods 5 and 6 aimed to get a clearer idea of what will be required of dietetics students in their future workplaces. The surveys revealed that the target needs of these students vary, and that these needs are usually delayed and often unexpected.

Regardless of that, however, they should all have a command of basic English dietetics and culinary arts terminology, topics not covered by general English courses in Japan. Furthermore, as more foreigners visit and reside in Japan, they will need advice from Japanese dietitians on issues such as diabetes and food allergies. In Fukuoka, the number of students and researchers from other Asian countries has been steadily increasing.

The data I collected told me that I needed to target the most pressing needs of my students. I found that just 20% of students, those who would like to transfer to a four-year university, should study EAP. Considering that the majority of students plan to become dietitians right after graduation, however, our main approach should be teaching English for Specific Occupational Purposes (ESOP), a sub-branch of English for Occupational Purposes (EOP) (see Basturkmen, 2010, p. 6).

The students' future workplaces are usually in Japan: However, they will have to describe their own food culture and ingredients in English (to clients with low Japanese-language proficiency) and translate the recipes provided by the Japanese dietitians from Japanese to English. Furthermore, substantial knowledge of international food culture is required in order to dispense nutritional advice to clients from various cultural backgrounds. To attain these objectives, my students need a command of English terminology. Many basic terms that dietitians frequently use for client communication, such as *allergy*, *diabetes*, *ferment*, or *condiment*, are not taught in high schools in Japan.

Curriculum (re)development. With the cooperation of the current core content teachers, the EFL curriculum was re-developed (see Tsuda, 2012).

Along with curriculum development, I interviewed potential part-time native-English-speaking teachers to explain our students' needs. From my previous experience as a part-time teacher, I knew that many part-time teachers worked in several schools every day, and some of them could not commit to one school. I sought out teachers who could make a strong commitment to our program.

Second Stage: Collaboration

Materials Development

According to Tomlinson (2011, pp. 10–13), the basic principles for second-language acquisition that are relevant to the development of materials for language teaching are (1) the perceived relevance of tasks by learners, and (2) exposure to language in authentic use.

During the initial period of trial and error, I used several Western and Japanese cookbooks written in English without doing any research or consulting with any core content teachers. I innocently believed that they must be "authentic" and that students would find them relevant and useful. I was wrong. I quickly learned that developing materials requires time and constant modification (see Graves, 1996, pp. 27–28). This critical incident became an ideal opportunity to collaborate with core content teachers and native English teachers.

First effort at ESOP material development. A British colleague at a local university was looking for assistance for a young Singaporean homemaker. She was looking for students who could assist her with grocery shopping and cooking local dishes because she had trouble in everyday communication. In response to her request, I organized a volunteer student group to help her out and teach her how to cook local dishes. For this project, our students communicated in English as lingua franca.

After the project, my students told me they wanted to have local recipe books written in English. Because English cookbooks describing local ingredients and condiments had not been previously published, I asked the chief culinary professor for help. The result was a collaboration between native- and Japanese English teachers and culinary professors to design a bilingual recipe book of traditional local dishes, called *Recipes of Fukuoka* (Tsuda, Matsukuma, & Caton, 2009). It has a bilingual glossary of ingredients and cooking techniques, so by using this book as a teaching resource, our students will gain exposure to authentic materials that are more relevant to their needs as well as develop lexical knowledge about culinary arts. We used photos and the students' first language in the cookbook and in culinary lessons to help them learn how to read and write the recipes more easily.

English recipe-writing contest. We introduced this activity in the class "ESOP for Dietitians" for second-year students, immediately before their internship. It is based on collaboration between a Japanese English teacher (first author, Tsuda), a native English teacher (second author, de Lint), and core content teachers. The students submitted English recipes. Later, the Japanese and native-English teachers cohosted a "best recipe" award ceremony attended by the student participants, with the dietetics professor and the culinary professor as special guests. It was conducted in English, and feedback was provided.

From 2011 to 2014, the only specific instruction for the contest was: "A favorite Japanese dish that I would like to share with guests from overseas." At the time, the only evaluator was a native-English teacher (the second author). After completing my needs analysis, I found that diabetics are the most frequent subjects of dietetic counseling; therefore, in 2015, "A recipe for diabetics" was added to the contest, and two more evaluators—a dietetics professor and a culinary professor—were invited (in addition to me) to provide more relevant advice for students who were preparing for their internships. Student evaluations showed that they regarded feedback from the four evaluators as very practical and useful.

Below is the summary of the first-prize-winner's note, translated by us:

> The main aim of English classes at high school was to prepare for entrance exams, and focus on rote memory. At college, I learned a lot of dietetic terminology in English. I was not good at English, but I felt it easier to follow, because the contents of English lessons have been taught in content classes. Regarding the 'Recipe Writing Contest,' I had difficulty because I had never written recipes in English, but gradually I got the knack. When I could not find an expression in English, I searched the Internet and asked teachers.

Critical Role of Expert Knowledge

Thanks to collaboration between core content teachers and an English teacher, this contest motivated students. Nation (2013, p. 126) argues that in EFL settings, if English is not really needed for subject matter study, the motivation levels in the English course are likely to be very low. Therefore, cooperation between the English teachers and the subject matter (core content) teachers is critical.

We began this contest for students, but it evolved into a valuable opportunity for teacher collaboration. Some of the English recipes that I awarded high points to were not necessarily well written from the viewpoint of nutrition science and/or culinary arts, but the valuable lesson I learned from this experience is that language teachers really do need the input of experts if we are to accurately assess content knowledge.

Reflection on Teacher Collaboration

Looking back on my 10 years at this college, I can see that my professional development moved gradually from being a highly autonomous EFL instructor to a highly engaged faculty member collaborating across disciplines. Now I am engaged in several collaborative works with core content teachers for classroom teaching and research. Based on a case study in Japan, Sturman (1992) listed the following factors that influence the effectiveness of team-teaching: personality, respect, attitude toward the project, language, time, discipline, student attitudes, and staffroom atmosphere. For the work described in this chapter, "respect" is the crucial factor. Without respect, we could not have accomplished these collaborative projects within a limited time schedule because the workload of professors is very heavy.

In this chapter, we have explored teachers' collaboration through a story of teacher development. By collaborating with other teachers, I have developed skills as a needs analyst, course developer, materials developer, and team member (Richards & Lockhart, 1996, pp. 99–100). Through collaboration, teachers can complement each other and develop programs to be more practical and valuable for students. As intercultural communicators, we need to actively collaborate across languages and disciplines. In this way, language teachers will serve as inspiring role models for students.

Akiko Tsuda is an associate professor at Nakamura Gakuen University.

Darcy de Lint is a part-time EFL instructor at Nakamura Gakuen University.

ACKNOWLEDGEMENTS

We thank Professors Matsuguma Miki and Yamato Takako for their great amount of support, especially with the English Recipe-Writing Contest.

This work was supported by JSPS KAKENHI Grant Number 23520736/2637052.

References

Basturkmen, H. (2010). *Developing courses in English for specific purposes*. London, England: Palgrave Macmillan.

Dudley-Evans, T., & St John, M. (1998). *Developments in English for specific purposes: A multidisciplinary approach*. Cambridge, England: Cambridge University Press.

Fukue, N. (2009, January 27). No brown bagging it for students. *Japan Times*. Retrieved from http://www.japantimes.co.jp/

Graves, K. (1996). A framework of course development process. In K. Graves (Ed.), *Teachers as course developers* (pp. 12–38). Cambridge, England: Cambridge University Press.

Long, M. H. (2005). Methodological issues in learner needs analysis. In M. H. Long (Ed.), *Second language needs analysis* (pp. 19–76). Cambridge, England: Cambridge University Press.

Nation, P. (2011). *What should every EFL teacher know?* Seoul, Korea: Compass Publishing.

Richards, J. C., & Lockhart, C. (1996). *Reflective teaching in second language classrooms*. Cambridge, England: Cambridge University Press.

Stewart, T., Sagliano, M., & Sagliano, J. (2002). Merging expertise: Promoting partnerships between language and content specialists. In J. Crandall & D. Kaufman (Eds.), *Content-based language instruction* (pp. 29–44). Alexandria, VA: TESOL.

Sturman, P. (1992). Team teaching: A case study from Japan. In D. Nunan (Ed.), *Collaborative language learning and teaching* (pp. 141–161). Cambridge, England: Cambridge University Press.

Tomlinson, B. (2011). Introduction: Principles and procedures of materials development. In B. Tomlinson (Ed.), *Material development in language teaching, second edition* (pp. 1–31). Cambridge, England: Cambridge University Press.

Tsuda, A. (2012). Developing an ESP course and materials for dietitians. *Professional and academic English, Journal of English for Specific Interest Group*, 39, 23–24, 29–30.

Tsuda, A., Matsukuma, N., & Caton, T. (2009). *Recipes of Fukuoka*. Fukuoka, Japan: Kaichosha.

Appendix

Prize award ceremony.

Boiled pork with japones sauce

Serve 1

14F610 Gomitsu Hitomi

[Ingredients]

- ◆ Pork loin ················· 50g
- ◆ Potato starch ··············· 10g
- ◆ *Maitake* mushroom ······· 30g
- ◆ Japanese radish ·········· 40g
- ◆ *Siso* ···························· 5g
- ◆ Leek ··························· 10g
- ◆ Lettuce ······················ 5g
- ◆ Radish sprout··············· 5g
- ◆ Tomato ······················ 30g
- ◆ *Ponzu* soy sauce·········· 15g

[Directions]

1. Dust the potato starch to pork, and parboil in hot water.
   Chill cold water, and wipe the water off the surface.
   Cut into bite-size pieces.
2. Parboil *maitake* in hot water, and wipe the water off the surface.
   Cut into bite-size pieces.
3. Grate Japanese white radish, drain with a sieve, and transfer into a bowl.
   Slice *siso* and leek into pieces, and mix them well.
4. Slice thin lettuce into 5mm pieces, and serve lettuce in a plate.
   Cut tomatoes into quarter slice.
   Arrange pork, *maitake* and tomato.
   Sprinkle radish sprout, grated Japanese radish.
   Pour on *ponzu* soy sauce to serve.

list	1	2	3	4	5	6	sum
unit	0.5	—	1.3	—	—	0.4	**2.2**

Calorie : 176kcal

Carbohydrate : 10.3g

Protein : 13.0g

Fat : 6.9g

Original unedited 1st Prize winner's work.

15

Students and Teachers Co-Researching Difficulties With Vocabulary in Academic Writing: A Case Study of Exploratory Practice

QIAO WANG AND DAVID DALSKY

You've made me so very happy. I'm so glad you came into my life!

This voice could be heard during the first day of class, but it was neither from a student nor a teacher. It was from the music of Blood, Sweat, and Tears.

Put "quality of life" before all else in the classroom.

This voice also echoed in our first class, but it was from no one present. These words come from Dick Allwright, the founder of Exploratory Practice (EP) (Allwright, 2003).

One of the goals of this narrative is to demonstrate that it may take a little blood, sweat, and tears for teachers and students to collaborate in the classroom to achieve a high "quality of life." The voices in this chapter emerged from our academic writing class and reflect on how we applied the principles of EP (Allwright & Hanks, 2009), a form of inclusive practitioner research. We highlight the unification of learning, teaching, and research, including the positioning of students as co-researchers.

Concretely, this took the shape of the following: 1) the teachers learning from the students what they would like to study and how they would like to study (including their subjective experiences with the learning process), 2) the students and teachers collaborating to replicate a study involving the effect of academic source texts on academic vocabulary use in the subsequent writing of an essay, and 3) the teachers modeling how to correctly write a research paper through their write-up of the replicated study.

Our aim in writing this narrative is to share a story of a successful collaboration between teachers and students co-researching difficulties with academic writing following the principles of EP. The overarching goal was to reach a level of mutual understanding that might help us realize a high-quality of classroom life for all participants.

Class Description

Our story began in a general academic English writing course for freshmen majoring in chemistry (around 40 students) in one of Japan's elite national universities. We, the instructors, were a teacher and a teaching assistant (TA). The main course teaching and learning objective was to thoroughly cover the basics of academic writing. Instruction included basic paragraph development, essay structure, and writing a short research paper.

As is typical in Japanese classrooms, the students were very reticent. So reticent, in fact, that we detected something suspicious—either the students were uninterested or there was a deeper cultural issue playing out. In an attempt to understand this puzzle, we asked the students to write what they expected our class to offer and post their comments on an online learning management system (LMS). Their responses indicated that many of them were interested in something closely related to their field of study, i.e., writing authentic academic papers in English. Our class, however, focused on English for General Academic Purposes (EGAP) (see Tajino, Dalsky, & Sasao, 2009), and we knew from experience that this subject would be too difficult for the students (Dalsky & Tajino, 2007). We decided therefore to give them a voice in determining the course content and explore with them potentially novel learning avenues involving collaboration and mutual understanding.

To guide us on this journey, we elected to use the pedagogical framework of Exploratory Practice. Through EP, we could engage in inclusive practitioner research by collaborating with our students as co-researchers. In what follows, we explain more about the nature of EP and how we put it into action.

Introduction to Exploratory Practice

In 1991, Dick Allwright, the principal founder of EP, was invited to teach practical classroom research in Brazil. At the time, he focused on delivering greater efficiency but soon realized that it was a "thoroughly misguided enterprise" (Allwright, 2003). He began to rethink practitioner research in terms of the social aspects of language teaching and learning, and this reformulation laid the foundation for EP (Allwright, 2003). According to Allwright and Lenzuen (1997, p. 73):

> EP is a name given to a sustainable way of carrying out classroom investigations which provide language teachers (and potentially learners also) with a systematic framework within which to define areas of language teaching that they wish to explore, to refine their thinking about them, and to investigate them further using classroom activities, rather than academic research techniques, as the investigative tools.

More specifically, Allwright (2003) set forth the principles of EP as follows:

1. Put "quality of life" first.

2. Work primarily to understand language classroom life.

3. Involve everybody.

4. Work to bring people together.

5. Work for mutual development.

6. Integrate the work for understanding into classroom practice.

7. Make the work a continuous enterprise.

In our case, we wanted the students to be fully involved as co-practitioners. We also wanted them to feel positive about learning academic writing through mutual understanding and collaboration. We interpreted "quality of life" in Principle 1 to mean an enjoyable classroom experience. Indeed, EP seemed to be the most suitable framework for our educational research endeavor.

EP in our Classroom

In his 2003 work, Allwright emphasized that when discussing phases of EP, "the biggest artificial distinction . . . is between two sets of processes: (1) taking action for understanding, and (2) working with emerging understandings." We proceed to tell our story by following these two processes.

Taking Action for Understanding

About midway through the course, we began a five-week-long research project, thinking that would be the most appropriate way to introduce EP and strive for mutual understanding between the teachers and the students. Because we wanted the students to play an active role from the beginning, we allowed them to choose additional course content they were interested in. As mentioned earlier, the students were eager to engage with authentic academic papers and therefore decided to choose an academic paper in their field for critical reading.

After attempting to read the research articles, however, their frustration was evident and not unexpected. We distributed a questionnaire asking what the students in general hoped to learn during the course. Much to our surprise, most students expressed their expectation to learn to "read and write" academic papers, quite a daunting task for freshmen. The following are some of their most telling voices:

❝ I want to write perfect research papers by myself. **❞**

❝ I would like to acquire how to write academic English paper. This is because I am going to write a thesis in English in the future. **❞**

❝ I would like to completely acquire the way to write academic papers. **❞**

❝ I want to be able to read and write academic sentences in English with almost no difficulties. **❞**

When asked if the course had so far lived up to their expectations, the students' answers were mostly "no." They attributed this failure mostly to themselves, because they had "not enough vocabulary" and "low English levels." We spent one lesson explaining how the students might have overlooked the gap between EGAP and English for Specific Academic Purposes (ESAP).

After this discussion, the students agreed they had been too ambitious at the beginning of the project, and that academic papers were far more difficult than they thought. The autonomous experience of selecting a primary source text in chemistry to read led the students to be more inquisitive about academic writing. They wanted to know more about what made academic writing so difficult. In the parlance of EP, according to Principle 2, both the students and teachers were prepared to take action for understanding.

We proceeded to integrate our collaborative effort for understanding into classroom practice (EP Principle 6). We brought students together (EP Principle 4) by forming eight teams, each with three to five members. A leader who was appointed by the members led the team in discussing their puzzles about academic writing, following the methodology of EP in English for Academic Purposes (EAP) settings (see Hanks, 2015).

Once they agreed on their puzzles, team leaders wrote them on the whiteboard (see Figure 1). The majority of the puzzles focused on academic vocabulary, and the following are some vocabulary-related quotes from students:

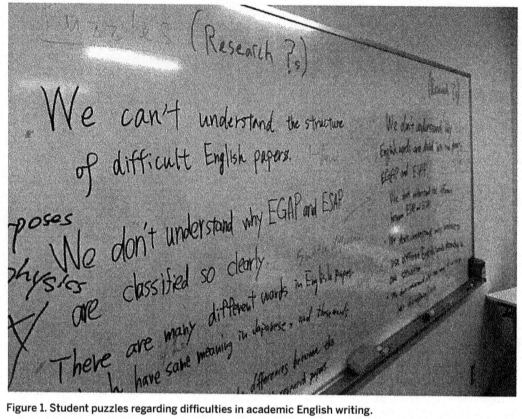

Figure 1. Student puzzles regarding difficulties in academic English writing.

> ❝ It [lack of vocabulary] really prevents us from reading smoothly. So many academic words. I forgot the first one when I was checking the second one. ❞

> ❝ Why do authors write 'ascertain' when they can use 'find out' that means the same? ❞

Up to this point, we had already reached understanding with the students regarding course content and their vocabulary difficulties in academic writing.

The remaining question for us was, "Should we go deeper?" To ensure that both students and teachers could reach mutual understanding to some degree, we asked the students where their puzzles were leading them. Was it a *why* question (why is academic vocabulary so difficult?) or a *how* question (how can we deal with it?)? Almost unanimously, the students said it was the latter. Therefore, the students phrased their final puzzle as, "How can our vocabulary use become more academic?"

Working With Emerging Understandings

Because there is already abundant literature in academic vocabulary use, we suggested the students search for relevant articles, papers, or even books and find out if there were similar situations. After doing critical reading, they brought their materials to their respective teams and discussed possible ways to understand their vocabulary puzzle with their team members. Not all materials were relevant, but some were very helpful. In one particular case study published in a reputable peer-reviewed journal, there were many quotes from students who were also troubled by academic vocabulary, and the author (Coxhead, 2012) used source texts to guide students in academic writing; the method proved useful in lexical choices.

The students in our class could empathize with the student voices in the case study and became curious if such a method could work for them as well. We also thought it would be a good idea to replicate this study, and, following the principles of EP, positioned the students as co-researchers by replicating the methods used in the Coxhead study.

First, the students read a source text on how the European Union was addressing climate change, and then they wrote a 500-word essay on the same issue. Climate change happened to be the topic in the Coxhead study, and it was suitable for our students because it was relevant to their field of study and still in the realm of EGAP. After finishing the essay, the students interviewed their partner(s) about the influence of the source text on vocabulary use in their essays and what they thought of such a writing method.

They then posted a few responses that they considered impressive on the online LMS, so that every student could see what others thought. In the end, after analyzing the results of the interview, they wrote their own conclusions about whether writing with a source text was useful in terms of academic vocabulary usage and supported their opinion with quotes from other students.

Finally, using the Coxhead (2012) model, the students wrote culminating reports about their replicated study, including the following parts: title, abstract, introduction, methods, results, conclusion and discussion, references, and appendices.

Reflections

The majority of the students considered writing from source texts to be a useful way for developing their academic writing skills. They also mentioned that the source texts would be most useful if they are optimally relevant to the writing topics and are current. Some students suggested that the teachers try this method in the future, whereas others said we should look at the bigger picture because there are likely other methods for expanding vocabulary use in academic writing. The sharing of these critical reflections was especially satisfying because everyone was actively involved.

The method in the Coxhead case study did not, of course, entertain all the individually unique puzzles the students had about academic vocabulary. According to the students' reports, however, we concluded with some degree of certainty that our EP practice was successful.

For one thing, the students took an active part in class activities and became obviously more positively engaged, especially as they worked together in teams. As a follow-up to our EP project, we asked the students to share their opinions about EP as a way to bring both teachers and students together and enhance the quality of life in the classroom. The following are some quotes from an end-of-semester questionnaire (see Appendix).

❝ In my group, we discussed about Mr. D's homework, and so on, and I could express my ideas. One of these ideas became our group's decision. ❞

❝ In other classes, all I have to do is to listen to teachers and understand what they want to say. On the other hand, in this class I have not only to listen to the teacher, but also to think about it myself and write or tell what I think. I think that this is the major differences. ❞

❝ I felt so happy to take this class. I could not only enjoy this class but also learn about academic English writing. Thanks to the class, I got interested in academic English. ❞

❝ I felt happy and sad in the same time because I felt happy to express my opinion, but sad to realized my English skill was low. ❞

From the students' responses, we can venture to say that the EP experience made them happier in the classroom, which we believe is the criterion of "quality of life." We further surmise that such happiness derived from our efforts to foster mutual understanding and collaboration, evidenced by peer assistance and teacher support in the process. Yet, it turned out that learner autonomy might have also played an important role. Many students mentioned the importance of their contributions to course decision making and appreciated the respect their voices were shown in our class. When they felt valued by the teachers and their classmates, their sense of responsibility towards group discussions, writing tasks, and peer interviews grew by leaps and bounds.

Conclusion

The important lesson we learned from the voices of all the participants was that there are sometimes gaps between students' expectations and course objectives. Instead of being viewed as a problem, however, such gaps can play a crucial role in lesson planning. Procedurally, this involves a flexible implementation of lesson plans that do not limit teachers to following a predetermined list of teaching points. Allwright (2005, p. 10) put it this way: "I see planning as crucial to language teaching and learning, but planning for richness of opportunity and especially for understanding, not planning to determine highly specific learning outcomes."

Our lesson planning was unexpectedly shifted by the Japanese students' voices that emerged through EP participant research. Their input enriched course content and enabled us to steer the class toward what students said they considered an engaging and enjoyable atmosphere. Had we not solicited their voices, we would have simply followed the teaching points and blamed the students' passivity on the "typical characteristics of Japanese students." We learned that having a flexible plan and giving students input into the plan enriches the quality of classroom life and increases the level of student engagement.

Upon further reflection, we realized that the students participated in our common exploration mostly through writing. We were unaware that our Japanese students would be better off thinking in silence rather than thinking through other means, until grappling with the relevant literature (e.g., Kim, 2002; Nakane, 2006). These students are silent for a psychological reason namely, they are conditioned to respect teachers as authority figures with their silence.

In other words, their silence speaks loudly about their level of respect. Teachers should therefore encourage Japanese students to articulate any expectations and difficulties related to the class through culturally appropriate ways of self-expression, not necessarily in an audible form. In our case, the students' written voices encouraged their more active involvement in classroom life. Our inclusive participant inquiry through EP opened up new learning opportunities that otherwise would have remained unseen by the teachers. The students' voices managed to turn our attention away from the busy chatter of our teaching points toward an unbounded search for mutual cultural understanding—situated, ironically, in the sound of silence.

Qiao Wang is a graduate student at Kyoto University in Japan.

David Dalsky is an associate professor at Kyoto University in Japan.

References

Allwright, D. (2003). Exploratory practice: Rethinking practitioner research in language teaching. *Language Teaching Research*, 7(2), 113–141. doi:10.1191/1362168803lr118oa

Allwright, D. (2005). From teaching points to learning opportunities and beyond. *TESOL Quarterly*, 39(1), 9–31. doi:10.2307/3588450

Allwright, D., & Hanks, J. (2009). *The developing language learner: An introduction to Exploratory Practice*. New York, NY: Palgrave Macmillan.

Allwright, D., & Lenzuen, R. (1997). Exploratory Practice: Work at the Cultura Inglesa, Rio de Janeiro, Brazil. *Language Teaching Research*, 1(1), 73–79.

Coxhead, A. (2012). Academic vocabulary, writing and English for academic purposes: Perspectives from second language learners. *RELC Journal*, 43(1), 137–145. doi: 10.1177/0033688212439323

Dalsky, D., & Tajino, A. (2007). Students' perceptions of difficulties with academic writing: A report from Kyoto University academic writing courses. *Kyoto University Researches in Higher Education*, 13, 45–51.

Hanks, J. (2015) 'Education is not just teaching': Learner thoughts on Exploratory Practice. *ELT Journal*, 69(2), 117–128. doi:10.1093/elt/ccu063

Kim, H. S. (2002). We talk, therefore we think? A cultural analysis of the effect of talking on thinking. *Journal of Personality and Social Psychology*, 83(4), 828.

Nakane, I. (2006). Silence and politeness in intercultural communication in university seminars. *Journal of Pragmatics*, 38(11), 1811–1835. doi:10.1016/j.pragma.2006.01.005

Tajino, A., Dalsky, D., & Sasao, Y. (2009). Academic vocabulary reconsidered: An EAP curriculum-design perspective. *Iranian Journal of Teaching English as a Foreign Language and Literature*, 4, 3–21.

Appendix

Please recall our academic writing course from the very beginning and answer the following questions. We would appreciate it if you can share honestly what you think of the course.

1. Do you think the teachers and students gradually reached mutual understanding during the past year?

2. Do you think there has been enough collaboration among students and also between teachers and students in the class?

3. Do you think you were involved in the class's decision-making process? Please state some of the examples.

4. How did you feel when you were taking the class? Were you happy, uninterested, or anything else?

5. What do you think are the major differences of this class compared with other classes you are taking?

16 Conclusion: Theorizing Forward on TESOL Classroom Practice

TIM STEWART

I n this chapter, I will lace together some of the main strands of current theory that is reflected in the practice described in this volume. TESOL is a diverse profession and understandably contains a plurality of voices, that is, discourses about theory and practice. Within this babble about pedagogical issues lay contemporary understandings of TESOL practice.

The current trend is captured by the TESOL International Association's most recent research agenda. In particular, it acknowledges the need for "increased emphasis on the agency of teachers as advocates for change inside and outside of their classrooms" (TESOL, 2014, p. 2). Advocacy is not a neutral or apolitical activity. It transpires out of the messy work of teachers making inquiries into their practice (Stewart, 2006, 2013). Schoolteachers might resist starting formalized inquiries, but without this experience, it is difficult for teachers to speak with authority in the never-ending education reform debate. The void created by the lack of authoritative teacher voices gets filled by loud voices from outside of classrooms pushing certain agendas (e.g., Meyer & Benavot, 2013). To push back against uninformed agendas, it's necessary for teachers to find their voices and uphold the research value in their own personal practical insider knowledge. Chapters in this book are examples of teacher-researchers raising their voices through descriptions of TESOL practice that illustrate the mutually informing nature of the theory-practice cycle.

Echoes of Classroom Research

Students as Co-researchers

Inviting the voices of students into discussions about curriculum and pedagogical approach is highlighted in several of the chapters in this book. This style of instruction is referred to as postmethods (Kumaravadivelu, 1994), which deemphasizes technique and foregrounds reflection. Three of the chapters (2, 5, and 16) introduce exploratory practice (Allwright, 2003) and show how students can become co-researchers and develop metacognitively. Dawson (Chapter 2) suggests that when students take more responsibility for their learning and are encouraged to ask questions, or form puzzles, about their language learning, the benefits are realized long after the course concludes.

By inviting students to become co-researchers into classroom activity, teachers position themselves as learners. This is important psychologically as a way to open up pedagogy to all participants. Haghi and Sharpling (Chapter 6) found a way to enrich their EAP course by experimenting with formative assessment practices that guide students toward learning targets. They recommend assessment *for* learning that involves all course participants.

Hassan and Nunn (Chapter 5) challenge Atkinson's (1997) contention that teaching critical thinking is burdened with cultural baggage and that the skill of thinking critically cannot be transferred. They agree with Le Ha (2004) that local values are not a "deficit" and should be integrated into curricula. This style of teaching practice follows Toth and Davin, who believe that ". . . maximizing pedagogical effectiveness requires thoroughly coming to know what counts as familiar territory for learners, and assessing how best to translate pedagogical novelty into experiences that connect meaningfully with prior knowledge" (2016, p. 150).

The accounts from West (Chapter 12) and Wang and Dalsky (Chapter 16) show how peer teaching can be used to involve students more in the process of learning. Both chapters describe students working through the process of academic writing. Looking through their own cultural filters, Wang and Dalsky first viewed the silence of their students as a deficit. After opening up their classroom through exploratory practice (Allwright, 2003), they learned the reasons behind the silence (Le Ha, 2004; Nakane, 2006) and this made all the difference.

Reverberation on Teacher Development and Collaboration

Developing our professional practice as teachers requires collaboration with students and other teachers. Kern (2014) asks teachers to consider how much they know about the lives of today's students. For instance, how much do language teachers know about what students need to learn in mainstream university classes (Kehe & Kehe, 1996)? Burghardt and Connolly (Chapter 4) wonder about this. Their students need to learn the culture of the American university. They advocate expanding Kern's (2000) categories for literacy (cognitive, linguistic, and cultural) to include technological. This is a worthy goal of practice, but in an age when the medium truly is the message, learning how students view communication and new technologies is critical. Kramsch (2014) describes the meaning of communication today as "restricted to communication for communication's sake" (p. 303). Molle and Prior (2008) show that the genres of academic writing are now multimodal. This implies that teachers need to stay current with research tools and skills (see Chun, Kern, & Smith, 2016). That is, teachers of academic writing should do academic writing.

Collaboration with subject-area faculty surely must be pursued if we are to find responses to the above challenges. Kırkgöz (Chapter 3) and Tsuda and de Lint (Chapter 15) sought out faculty in discipline areas to better meet the needs of their students. Kırkgöz introduced problem-based learning, which is not widely used in EAP courses (see Wood & Head, 2004). Her new approach drew praise from faculty and students in the engineering department. In their English for Occupational Purposes (EOP) course, Tsuda and de Lint collaborated extensively with dietitians to learn about how their students would need to use English on the job. Their chapter highlights how students might appreciate language learning as having exchange value—adding to their economic capital (Duchene & Heller, 2012). In addition, Tsuda's production of a local cookbook in English aligns with the larger issue of the hegemonic power of big Western publishers (see also Ngo & Nguyen in this volume). In order to maintain its dominant market hold, the global textbook industry is creating "global" books with some add-on features for specific markets (Kumaravadivelu, 2016).

Teachers can provide great educational service by building supportive frameworks in schools and local areas. Practitioners cannot develop alone. Ngo and Nguyen (Chapter 13) use student voices to point out challenges for teachers and students in listening classes in rural Vietnam. Their solution as Western-trained local teachers was to offer teacher-development workshops. Second-language teacher education programs now use models that encourage teachers to examine their own values and beliefs about teaching and learning. Collaboration with peers is held up as an important part of the process of developing a professional identity. In the view of Bill Johnston (2009), "Collaborative teacher development is not an add-on luxury for rare cases, but a vital component of any healthy, forward-looking educational setting" (p. 246).

Johnston's point helps us to unify the need for collaboration in teacher development that includes classroom research. Nonnative-English-speaking teachers (NNESTs) have lived with the stress of marginalized status for a long time (Kumaravadivelu, 2016; Phillipson, 2009). Rie Smithers (Chapter 14) is a nonnative-English-speaking teacher who sought to develop as a practitioner by engaging in classroom research for the first time. As a novice in this type of research, she collaborated with her husband, who served as an expert guide. This type of mentoring collaboration seems to be necessary as an incentive for many classroom teachers to start researching their practice (Chun, 2016; Yuan, Sun, & Teng, 2016). Smithers and Smithers present a compelling picture of how teachers in EFL contexts often struggle with alien pedagogical styles that have been imported along with the ideology of neoliberalism.

Narrating Identity

The social approach of learning as identity construction (Norton, 2000) has added rich dimensions to research on TESOL practice. On the teaching side, we need to know our own stories and the educational values that drive our practice. Khasnabis, Ambrosino, Sajjadi, and Reischl (Chapter 7) share their learner stories and reflect on how experience has shaped their teaching practices. They found that creating their own cultural autobiographies as newcomers to the United States sensitized them as teachers. Interaction in classrooms is influenced by complex social relations. "Thus, the quantity and quality of learner language often reflects attempts to project or suppress features of learners' identities, or to protect or alter their perceived social status" (Toth & Davin, 2016, p. 151). Khasnabis et al. believe that storytelling and story listening can form the core of language courses (see Freadman, 2014).

Talalakina and Grigoryeva (Chapter 9) engage their identities in discussion about the current needs of Russian EFL students. Their teacher-student dialogue raises interesting questions about how to approach developing competencies in English that are alien to other cultures (Canagarajah, 2016). Their positioning of English instruction in Russian universities as English as an International Language reflects part of the debate in the field on target language (Canagarajah, 2007; Pennycook, 2008). Kramsch (2014) describes the contemporary foreign language landscape as a competition in which English is winning against all other languages. While Talalakina and Grigoryeva contend that young Russians need to create global identities in order to engage in global conversations, Kramsch frets about the gap between

> . . . a global culture of communication for the sake of communication and local cultures of shared values. The tension between these two ways of conceiving of communication, negotiation, and meaning increases the communicative gap between generations and between teachers and their students. (2014, p. 302)

Kramsch is expressing concern about the loss of authenticity of languages as the Internet closes the distance between different languages and cultures (see Kern, 2014). Online exchanges are increasingly hybrid in character. Blommaert (2010, p. 103) refers to this trend as "truncated multilingualism." Firth, Broadbridge, and Siegel (Chapter 11) see studying abroad as a transformative learning experience that has the potential to expand students' individual identities. The voices of their students make clear they need more support to develop pragmatic speaking skills (Taguchi, 2012). Their practice highlights the work of language socialization scholars who emphasize that most learning takes place outside of classrooms (Duff & Talmy, 2011). Canagarajah says: "Socialization models suggest how learners can constructively interact with their peers and their mentors to develop their identities and communicative resources with greater agency in ways relevant to their social functions" (2016, p. 20).

Strong (Chapter 8) and Takeda (Chapter 10) both focus on cultural learning in their English classes. Strong uses autoethnography (Adams, Jones, & Ellis, 2015) together with Hofstedes's (1991) categories for analyzing dimensions of culture. He and his students use Hofstede's model to question aspects of culture. Takeda has her students reflect on the stereotypes they hold through letter exchanges with Cambodian students. These reflections on culture and identity stand in contrast to claims that young adults today are far more interested in commenting than in negotiating meanings (Kern, 2014).

Magnan, Murphy, and Sahakyan (2014) go further and argue that students today see intercultural communication as predominantly oral and do not value cross-cultural comparison. If this is true, it might be due to the process in liberal multiculturalism of essentializing and ignoring differences (Kubota, 2004). The students in Takeda's and Strong's courses did learn something about their home culture through intercultural reflection. What they found was that developing a unique voice requires attuning their ears to be more empathetic toward others (see Kramsch, 2014).

Cultivating Diverse Voices: Emancipating TESOL Classroom Stories

As reflected in this volume, the main plot of stories about second-language classroom practice today is one of collaboration—between colleagues inside and outside of classrooms and between all of the participants who take part in lessons. A key demand on teachers today is to engage in classroom inquiry that involves sharing stories about learning. This process of inquiry can be understood through the concept of pedagogical content knowledge (Shulman, 1987). In a recent elaboration of this concept, Ball, Thames, and Phelps (2008) assert that teachers need to have knowledge of content and teaching, as well as knowledge of how content is made appropriate for a range of students. This complex process requires a team-learning approach (see Tajino & Smith, 2016) in which all participants negotiate their purposes for learning within domains of knowledge. This inclusive, reflexive stance recognizes the tension between a lesson as a written plan and a lesson as an interactive event. Toth and Davin (2016) argue that teachers can resolve this inherent tension by becoming more responsive to learner needs during their classroom lesson performances.

When first conceiving this series of six books, opinions about chapter format were exchanged amongst the volume editors. While some wanted me to create a prescriptive template, I decided instead to offer authors a general set of guidelines to help them write their chapters. Our image for the series was something experimental and innovative. Most authors, however, struggled to narrate their classroom stories with authentic voices.

Freeman (1986) has long argued that second-language teachers need to find their own indigenous ways of writing what they know about teaching practice. His warning against adapting the approaches of empirical studies when writing up research is loudly echoed by Canagarajah, who claims that intellectual space needs to be opened by journal editors and reviewers for "a straightforward narrative as a research genre" (2016, p. 30). He reinforces this point by explaining how scholars in fields such as anthropology and sociology "are able to present autoethnographies that don't engage explicitly with published literature, citations, or research methods" (p. 30). In response to research guidelines published for the *TESOL Quarterly* in 2004, Shohamy (2004) and Holliday (2004) questioned the need for both strict research design prescriptions and reporting structures. Shohamy observes:

> Should researchers not rethink the order of *purpose of the research, literature review, rationale, research questions, design*, and so forth? Researchers have followed this structure for a long time. Is this really the best and most convincing way to present research? (p. 729)

Unfortunately, 12 years later, many authors for this volume were reluctant to experiment with more creative genres, which is likely the fault of my decision to create general chapter guidelines. For many authors this was a missed opportunity, mainly because it distorts the actual practice as experienced by the participants. It is clear to me that more multimodal approaches (Early, Kendrick, & Potts, 2015) need to be promoted for displaying knowledge.

Finally, the influence of technology and the Internet is ubiquitous. This fact cannot be ignored when thinking about the future of TESOL classroom practice in higher education. The Internet is more insidious than film or television at displaying propaganda. Furthermore, the information we see online is often filtered by algorithms designed so that we are less likely to be exposed to information that challenges us or broadens our perspective. This process is what Eli Pariser calls *The Filter Bubble* (2011).

The role of teachers in this digital information environment should be to help their students decode the images, sounds, and text they are bombarded by daily. "The more real-world communication takes place in the virtual world of networked computers, the more crucial it becomes for instructional environments not to emulate the computer, but to offer precisely what the computer cannot do, namely, reflect critically on its own symbolic and virtual realities" (Kramsch, 2009, p. 194). What this calls for is a greater focus on media literacy skills (Egbert & Neville, 2015; Quinlisk, 2003; Valentine & Wukovitz, 2013). In addition to developing their grammar, vocabulary, and knowledge of pragmatics and genres, language learners also need to develop a disposition for paying critical attention to the culturally encoded connections among forms, contexts, meanings, and ideologies in a variety of material mediums (Chun, Kern, & Smith, 2016, p. 66).

TESOL educators are well positioned to use their sensitivity to students and their own creativity to build into their courses the skills that get students questioning what they see, hear, and read.

Our basic goal as TESOL practitioners in higher education is literacy—to allow our students to learn and communicate their opinions and ideas in English. Students in our classrooms engage with English through their identities and aspirations. They learn how to appropriate the voices of the imagined communities they aspire to join. The ability of teachers to promote learner agency is crucial to how our students develop their identities as users of English together with their distinctive voices. An important way TESOL educators can foster this development is by guiding students on how to examine different perspectives through a critical eye. Then our students will become informed citizens who can raise their voices in the crucial debates about the types of societies we wish to create together.

....

Tim Stewart is an associate professor of TESOL at Kyoto University and the series editor of the six-volume series, *TESOL Voices*.

References

Adams, T. E., Jones, S. H., & Ellis, C. (2015). *Autoethnography*. Oxford, England: Oxford University Press.

Allwright, D. (2003). Exploratory practice: Rethinking practitioner research in language teaching. *Language Teaching Research, 7*(2), 113–141. doi:10.1191/1362168803lr118oa

Atkinson, D. (1997). A critical approach to critical thinking in TESOL. *TESOL Quarterly, 31*(1), 71–94.

Ball, D. L., Thames, M. H., & Phelps, G. (2008). Content knowledge for teaching: What makes it special? *Journal of Teacher Education, 59*, 389–407.

Blommaert, J. (2010). *The sociolinguistics of globalization*. Cambridge, England: Cambridge University Press.

Canagarajah, S. (2007). Lingua franca English, multilingual communities, and language acquistion. *Modern Language Journal, 91*, 921–937. doi:10.1111/j.1540-4781.2007.00678.x

Canagarajah, S. (2016). TESOL as a professional community: A half-century of pedagogy, research, and theory. *TESOL Quarterly, 50*(1), 7–41. doi:10.1002/tesq.275

Chun, C. W. (2016). Addressing racialized multicultural discourses in an EAP textbook: Working toward a critical pedagogies approach. *TESOL Quarterly, 50*(1), 109–131. doi:10.1002/tesq.216

Chun, D., Kern, R., & Smith, B. (2016). Technology in language use, language teaching, and language learning. *The Modern Language Journal, 100*(Supplement 2016), 64–80. doi:10.1111/modl.123020026-7902/16/64-80

Duchene, A., & Heller, M. (Eds.). (2012). *Language in late capitalism*. New York, NY: Routledge.

Duff, P. A., & Talmy, S. (2011). Language socialization approaches to second language acquisition: Social, cultural, and linguistic development in additional languages. In D. Atkinson (Ed.), *Alternative approaches to second language acquisition* (pp. 94–116). Abingdon, England: Routledge.

Early, M., Kendrick, M., & Potts, D. (2015). Multimodality: Out from the margins of English language teaching. *TESOL Quarterly, 49*(3), 447–460. doi:10.1002/tesq.246

Egbert, J., & Neville, C. (2015). Engaging K–12 language learners in media literacy. *TESOL Journal, 6*(1), 177–187. doi:10.1002/tesj.182

Freadman, A. (2014). Fragmented memory in a global age: The place of storytelling in modern language curricula. *Modern Language Journal, 98*(1), 373–385. doi:10.1111/j.1540-4781.2014.12067.x

Freeman, D. (1986). Redefining the relationship between research and what teachers know. In K. M. Bailey & D. Nunan (Eds.), *Voices from the language classroom* (pp. 88–115). Cambridge, England: Cambridge University Press.

Hofstede, G. (1991). *Cultures and organisations: Software of the mind*. Berkshire, England: McGraw Hill.

Holliday, A. (2004). Issues of validity in progressive paradigms of qualitative research. *TESOL Quarterly, 38*(4), 731–734.

Johnston, B. (2009). Collaborative teacher development. In A. Burns & J. C. Richards (Eds.), *The Cambridge guide to second language teacher education* (pp. 241–249). New York, NY: Cambridge University Press.

Kehe, D., & Kehe, P. (1996). Professors' expectations of foreign students in freshman-level courses. *JALT Journal*, *18*(1), 108–115.

Kern, R. (2000). *Literacy and language teaching*. Oxford, England: Oxford University Press.

Kern, R. (2014). Technology as *Pharmakon*: The promise and perils of the Internet for foreign language education. *Modern Language Journal*, *98*(1), 340–357. doi:10.1111/j.1540-4781.2014.12065.x

Kramsch, C. (2009). *The multilingual subject*. Oxford, England: Oxford University Press.

Kramsch, C. (2014). Teaching foreign languages in an era of globalization: Introduction. *Modern Language Journal*, *98*(1), 296–311. doi:10.1111/j.1540-4781.2014.12057.x

Kubota, R. (2004). Critical multiculturalism and second language education. In B. Norton & K. Toohey (Eds.), *Critical pedagogies and language learning* (pp. 30–52). New York, NY: Cambridge University Press.

Kumaravadivelu, B. (1994). The postmethod condition: (E)merging strategies for second/foreign language teaching. *TESOL Quarterly*, *28*(1), 27–48. doi:10.2307/3587197

Kumarravadivelu, B. (2016). The decolonial option in English teaching: Can the subaltern act? *TESOL Quarterly*, *50*(1), 66–85. doi:10.1002/tesq.202

Le Ha, P. (2004). University classrooms in Vietnam: Contesting the stereotypes. *ELT Journal*, *58*(1), 50–57.

Magnan, S. S., Murphy, D., & Sahakyan, N. (2014). Goals of collegiate learners and the Standards for Foreign Language Learning. *Modern Language Journal*, *98*, Supplement.

Meyer, H. D., & Benavot, A. (Eds.). (2013). *PISA, power, and policy: The emergence of global educational governance*. Oxford, England: Symposium Books.

Molle, D., & Prior, P. (2008). Multimodal genre systems in EAP writing pedagogy: Reflecting on a needs analysis. *TESOL Quarterly*, *42*, 541–566. doi:10.1002/j.1545-7249.2008.tb00148x

Nakane, I. (2006). Silence and politeness in intercultural communication in university seminars. *Journal of Pragmatics*, *38*(11), 1811–1835. doi:10.1016/j.pragma.2006.01.005

Norton, B. (2000). *Identity and language learning: Gender, ethnicity and educational change*. Harlow, England: Pearson Education.

Pariser, E. (2011). *The filter bubble: What the Internet is hiding from you*. New York, NY: Penguin.

Pennycook, A. (2008). Multilithic Englishes and language ideologies. *Language in Society*, *37*, 435–444.

Phillipson, R. (2009). *Linguistic imperialism continued*. London, England: Routledge.

Quinlisk, C. C. (2003). Media literacy in the ESL/EFL classroom: Reading images and cultural stories. *TESOL Journal*, *12*(3), 35–39. doi:10.1002/j.1949-3533.2003.tb00141.x

Shohamy, E. (2004). Reflections on research guidelines, categories, and responsibilities. *TESOL Quarterly*, *38*(4), 728–731.

Shulman, L. (1987). Knowledge and teaching: Foundations of the new reform. *Harvard Educational Review*, *57*, 1–22.

Stewart, T. (2006). Teacher-researcher collaboration or teachers' research? *TESOL Quarterly*, *40*(2), 421–430. doi:10.2307/40264529

Stewart, T. (2013). *Classroom research for language teachers*. Alexandria, VA: TESOL Press.

Taguchi, N. (2012). *Context, individual differences, and pragmatic competence*. New York, NY: Multilingual Matters.

Tajino, A., & Smith, C. (2016). Beyond team teaching: An introduction to team learning in language education. In A. Tajino, T. Stewart, & D. Dalsky (Eds.), *Team teaching and team learning in the language classroom* (pp. 11–27). New York, NY: Routledge.

TESOL. (2014). *Research agenda*. Alexandria, VA: Author. Retrieved from http://www.tesol.org

Toth, P. D., & Davin, K. J. (2016). The sociocognitive imperative of L2 pedagogy. *The Modern Language Journal, 100*(Supplement 2016), 148–168. doi:10.1111/modl.123060026-7902/16/148-168

Valentine, A., & Wukovitz, L. (2013). A case study utilizing online personalization to engage students in information literacy instruction. *Research & Practice, 1*(1), 24–34. doi:10.5195/palrap.2013.18

Wood, A., & Head, M. (2004). 'Just what the doctor ordered': The application of problem-based learning to EAP. *English for Specific Purposes, 23*, 3–17.

Yuan, R., Sun, P., & Teng, L. (2016). Understanding language teachers' motivations towards research. *TESOL Quarterly, 50*(1), 220–234. doi:10.1002/tesq.279